D1558657

THE MIRACLE POWER
OF BELIEVING

Faith is to believe what we do not see; and the reward of this faith is to see what we believe.

St. Augustine

THE MIRACLE POWER
OF BELIEVING

Theodor Laurence

Parker Publishing Company, Inc.
West Nyack, N.Y.

For Gretchen L., who wants to know.

© 1976, by

Theodor Laurence

*All rights reserved. No part of this
book may be reproduced in any form
or by any means, without permission
in writing from the author.*

Library of Congress Cataloging in Publication Data

Laurence, Theodor.
    The miracle power of believing.

    1. Success. 2. Apostles' Creed-Miscellanea.
3. Creeds--Miscellanea. I. Title.
BJ1611.2.L4   248'.4   75-35831
ISBN 0-13-585810-0

Printed in the United States of America

What This Book Will Do For You

It struck me more than once over the past twenty years that people unwittingly and often erroneously use a certain inner power in their lives. This latent power is the Power of Belief. But more often than not, this miraculous power is misused or misapplied.

For instance, I began to notice early that many people are bombarded by worries and anxieties, deprivation, lack of money, personal setbacks and trials, and many other life-consuming things. And I noted that many of these people were suffering these things *because they believed in them.* * That was the key to this book.

I began to realize that if people could bring bad luck and illness and depression upon themselves by the sheer act of belief, then conversely, they could also bring joy and happiness into their lives if they believed in these things.

It became clear to me as I watched more and more people that there are some individuals who are capable of greatly enhancing their own lives simply by activating their power of belief. It also became clear that too many people have forgotten how to believe, for they have been subdued by modern rapid changes, the vastness of big business and the shock of cultural shifts. Individuality, I saw, was being slowly filtered out in favor of group effort and herd behavior. Consequently, people were suffering lack and poverty when all around them and from within them there is abundance, wealth and glory.

---

* For insight into the dangers of the *Negative* use of the power of belief, see *Satan, Sorcery and Sex*.

THE RESURRECTION OF THE POWER OF BELIEF

I determined to find out just what part the power of belief plays in life. In time I was honored to see that the power of belief can work miracles, for this power is a latent, dormant and psychic power. It became obvious to me that the power of belief puts you in touch with remarkable sources of power, love, money, riches, wealth, happiness and success. But the power of belief has to be triggered, set free and unleashed. My religious experiences reminded me of the power of the Apostle's Creed. My psychological knowledge reminded me of the great and awesome Unconscious. When these two mighty concepts were wedded it was my extreme pleasure to see a remarkable change occur in the lives of those who used them as directed. I was surprised and amazed at the outstanding results these people achieved. Now this book is designed to bring you the secrets to all the things in life you want.

THE KEY TO MAGIC PERSONAL CREEDS

The power of belief, when activated and used, infuses a creed with life and vitality, which in turn alerts the powerful Unconscious to your needs. The following chapters of this book contain many potent creeds, based upon the Apostle's Creed, but updated, reformed, and energized to tap your inner source of plenty.

With the belief-activated magic personal creeds, otherwise average people achieved outstanding results, attained wealth, happiness, health, joy and even fun. They were able to control others, free themselves from domination, overcome illness and disease—*without moving a muscle*.

With the Power of Belief and Magic Personal Creeds you don't have to work, struggle, grunt or groan. You simply reactivate your Power of Belief and—this is the amazing thing!—the all-powerful Unconscious goes to work *for you!*

HOW YOU CAN JOIN THE THOUSANDS OF OTHERS LIKE YOURSELF WHO HAVE ENJOYED MIRACLES THROUGH THE USE OF THE POWER OF BELIEF AND PERSONAL CREEDS

People all over the country who had no other way to obtain the fulfillment of their wishes, dreams, and desires have successfully and happily used the

Power of Belief and the Magic of Personal Creeds. Here are some examples
of highly satisfied people:

1. How retiree Bert S. saved an estimated $1380 when he used
   the dynamic Love Creed. (See page 56.)
2. How Sandra K. changed from a high-strung, nervous
   young lady into a rock of strength when she practiced the
   Higher Self Creed. (See page 25.)
3. How Andy S., a two-dollar-an-hour office clerk, was promoted to a $750-a-month managerial position after using
   the miraculous Sustenance Creed. (See page 93.)
4. How Benjamin T., overworked and underpaid, *believed*
   himself into a $200-a-week job. (See page 140.)
5. How the Magnetism Creed drew all the luxuries Patrick F.
   wanted in life, even though he was earning a bus driver's
   wages. (See page 120.)
6. How June P. was transformed from a nagging housewife
   into a powerful helpmate overnight by using the Abundance Creed. (See page 182.)
7. How the Harmony Creed helps police officer Leo K. to
   reconcile people's differences so that he doesn't have to
   arrest them. (See page 150.)
8. How Mrs. Anthony P. got her new home in the middle of a
   financial crisis through her use of the Joy Creed. (See page
   36.)
9. How the Truth Creed made William R. a singing sensation
   overnight. (See page 38.)
10. How Sam V. won the heart of a woman from another man
    by using the Victory Creed. (See page 134.)
11. How lonely bachelor Glenn L. acquired more women than
    he could handle when he used the Purity Creed. (See page
    102.)
12. How the Progress Creed turned James L.'s insignificant
    job into a launching pad to success. (See page 163.)
13. How Andrew T. used the Guardianship Creed like a
    mighty sword to end the attack of negativity he was experi-
    encing and suffering. (See page 115.)
14. How underpaid secretary Barbara L. practiced the Good
    Fortune Creed and discovered a miraculous way to earn
    $250 per week. (See page 52.)
15. How Jeff T. overcame apathy and achieved fame and
    fortune with the Cosmic Power Creed. (See page 109.)
16. How Joe K. used the Self-Confidence Creed and moved

HOW THIS BOOK WILL HELP YOU
DO THE SAME—*AND MORE!*

Know definitely and with the utmost assurance that if you follow the clear, easy-to-use instructions in this book to reactivate your latent Power of Belief, you will be the recipient of love, riches, happiness, and success through the use of dynamic and miracle-producing Personal Creeds. You will experience the joy and fullness of life that the above people are experiencing as they continue to use the magic of Personal Creeds.

Nothing is required of you except your hidden potential. Permit the following creeds to activate and animate your inner powers and magic miracles will delight, heal and fulfill you. Let the magic happen to you, too, by following the steps outlined in this book and by applying the creeds to your daily life. You will excel. You will sigh with relief. You will laugh for joy. You will be amazed at what you can do, what you can be and what you can have. Fulfillment and success are here at your fingertips. All you have to do is turn the pages.

Theodor Laurence

If you wish to know a truth
To save yourself grief:
The secret to Life
Is the Power of Belief.

To know of many things
Is to know a clever thief;
To seek your own center
Is the Power of Belief.

From the Book of Life's pages
You must choose a single leaf;
'Tis done by the faithful
Through the Power of Belief.

Theodor Laurence

Contents

    STRIFE AND DISCORD 147

    Believing in Harmony Explodes Distress   147
    How the Harmony Creed Helped 43 Men at Once   148
    Some Testimonials from Harmonious People   149
    The Creed That Annihilates Fear and Stress   150
    How JFK Sued for Peace and Harmony   151
    Harmony Is Its Own Reward   151
    He Said: "Since I Started Using the Harmony Creed I've Made
        Over $50,000"   152
    How the Harmony Creed Produces That Alpha State   153
    The Many Uses of the Harmony Creed   153
    Let the Harmony Creed Help You   154
    How a New York Woman Developed Psychic Ability and Saved
        Her Own Life   154
    What the Higher Self Has in Store for You   156
    They Do Remarkable Things with ESP   157
    The Telepathic Child of Mrs. Skutch   157
    How a Young Man Discovered a Hidden Treasure   158
    How to Experience the Joy of Fulfillment and Success   159

18. HOW THE PROGRESS CREED TURNS YOUR MISFORTUNE
    INTO OPPORTUNITY 160

    The Difference Between Collective Progress and Individual
        Progress   160
    Learn the Difference and Move Forward to Victory   161
    The Creed That Awakens Your Sleeping Genie   161
    He Was Failing Because He Didn't Know He Could
        Succeed   162
    He Thought His Job Was Too Insignificant   163
    Independence and Progress Go Hand in Hand   166
    How He Emerged Triumphant from Corporate
        Materialism   166
    Become a Self-Starter   168
    They Didn't Know How Good He Was Until He Spoke
        Up   169
    How You Can Rise Above Misfortune and Adversity   171

1

How Personal Creeds Can Bring You Greater Rewards in Life

One of the oldest, most powerful creeds known to Western man is The Apostles' Creed. It shall be our prototype throughout this book, partly because it is the most familiar to the largest number of readers, and partly because, when properly employed as an exercise in self-actualization rather than a statement of articles of faith, it can serve as a dynamic system in your quest for the better things in life. How it can so serve you is the subject of this chapter.

Not everyone believes in the articles of faith contained in The Apostles' Creed, which is understandable, since not everyone is Christian. However, it has been my experience that this potent creed has helped many people develop their latent or depotentiated power of belief. One such person, Leon P., of Mount Vernon, New York, is illustrative of what I mean.

HOW AN ATHEIST UTILIZED THE APOSTLES' CREED

Leon came to me with a problem which is familiar to many of us today. His life seemed barren. His job was boring. His bills were mounting faster than he could pay them off. The very vitality of life itself seemed to have seeped away for him. He was listless and depressed, almost hopeless. I say almost because Leon came to discover what he could about correcting his situation. After a few hours of interview I diagnosed this young man as a person who had gotten out of touch with his own power of belief. When I suggested this to Leon, he immediately recognized the fact and admitted that he lacked faith in anything these days.

He said: "I gave up believing in anything a long time ago. I decided that if I was going to get anything out of this life, I'd have to take it."

We discussed his negative attitude at length, and I slowly moved the conversation to the empowering capacity of creeds in general and the Apostles' Creed in particular. Leon looked incredulous, and said, "I don't believe in God. I'm an atheist. I was born Jewish, so I sure don't believe in Christ. Why would I want to say the Apostles' Creed?"

I said, "I am not suggesting you adopt the creed as an expression of religious attitude, but rather as a spiritual and psychological method of developing your own power of belief. Your power has to be reactivated, set free, liberated. It's festering inside you and doing you no good. Each of us has the ability to employ that power, to put it to work for ourselves. The power of belief can brighten your whole life."

Leon grew quite interested and I explained to him that this creed is an effective device for rekindling one's dormant power of belief, the power necessary if one is to achieve, accomplish, receive. Paraphrasing Aristotle, who said: "He who wishes to learn must believe," I said to Leon: "He who wishes to receive must believe."

There was no doubt that Leon wanted the good things of life, so I explained to him that if he was going to get them he would first have to employ his power of belief. I introduced him to the Apostles' Creed as a workable method for developing his own power.

I said: "The Apostles' Creed can help you recharge your own repressed power of belief, no matter what its words say. The idea is to stress certain key words in it, words to which your inner power will respond."

I showed Leon the key words and he began reciting the Apostles' Creed daily, stressing these words as I had instructed him to do. It came as no surprise to me when, two weeks later, a bright-eyed, enthusiastic Leon came to visit me. He was laughing. He was animated. Life, he told me, had taken a turn for him. It was *alive*, he said. His job now interested him greatly. He had gotten a raise, from $2.50 per hour to $4.25 per hour, and this because he had taken a greater interest in his work. Once again, I saw for myself what the power of belief can do in the life of an individual.

Leon had taken the time and energy to suspend his unbelief long enough to give my creed-system a try. He had uttered the Apostles' Creed nightly, with feeling, stressing the key words. Here is the way I gave the creed to Leon. Stress the italicized words and after a few tries you will feel, not faith in the words, but an inner stirring, the reactivation of your power of belief.

THE CREED THAT TAPS YOUR LATENT POWER OF BELIEF

I *believe* in God the Father Almighty, Maker of heaven and earth:

And in Jesus Christ his only Son our Lord: Who was conceived by the Holy Ghost, Born of the Virgin Mary: Suffered under Pontius Pilate, Was crucified, dead, and buried: He descended into hell; The third day he rose again from the dead: He ascended into heaven, And sitteth on the right hand of God the Father Almighty: From thence he shall come to judge the quick and the dead.

I *believe* in the Holy Ghost: The holy Catholic Church; The

Communion of Saints: The Forgiveness of sins: The Resurrec-
tion of the body: and the Life everlasting.
Amen.

"Amen" means "so be it." It is your reaffirmation of belief. You reaffirm the existence of your *power of belief*, not the contents or meaning of the creed.

CREEDS THAT CAN BRING YOU HEALTH, WEALTH, POWER, AND PRESTIGE

Laura T., of Las Vegas, Nevada, insisted that she could not in all good conscience repeat the words of the Apostles' Creed. Unlike Leon, she could not bring herself to utter this creed with the conviction required. Laura was of spiritualistic leanings, so I gave her a creed which is based on the Apostles' Creed, but which uses different terminology. I reiterated that the words are not what is important, but the reaffirmation of your own power of belief. To demonstrate I gave Laura a creed based on her own spiritual proclivities. I explained to her that creeds are points of contact. A creed puts you in touch with higher forces, transcendent reality and superpersonal agencies. I assured Laura that she need not use traditional language.

I said, "Belief is assent; faith is consent and infers consecration. When you activate your power of belief, you commit yourself to the intervention of higher than human forces. Those forces may be called God, Self, Cosmic Power, Universal Mind, and what have you, but the name changes nothing."

In his profound book, *How to Believe,* Dr. Ralph W. Sockman says: "When we say, 'I believe in God,' we mean that we believe in God enough to trust him and commit our way to him."

Due to her personal experiences in childhood and early youth, Laura was unable to do this. She actually shuddered at the thought of praying. And yet when I prepared a creed based on the Apostles' Creed for her, she was willing and able to use it in daily practice. In the end she awakened her sleeping power of belief and acquired the very thing she wanted out of life: true love. Here is the creed Laura uses even today:

THE UNIVERSAL MIND CREED THAT WORKS MIRACLES

I *believe* in Universal Mind the Origin of All, Matrix of noumena and phenomena:

And in Creation its ultimate purpose: which was first in Thought, born of Love: suffered under human ignorance, was defiled, polluted, and ravished: it declined into chaos; in latter times it commanded reverence: it overawed man, and holds the promise of Life through Universal Mind the Origin of All: from thence it shall preserve the caring and the loving.

I *believe* in Mother Nature: the holiness of Life; the respect for Earth: the correction of ignorance: the replenishment of the Earth: and in Universal Mind beneficent.

Amen.

HOW HER POWER OF BELIEF MADE HER DREAM COME TRUE

Laura was able to identify with the words in the Universal Mind Creed. She was an ecologist at heart and these words touched her. I might point out to you that the true love Laura was seeking and despairing of was found in an ecology class! She and her new beau Ted M. attended every subsequent lecture which I gave in Los Angeles. That series was on "The Effects of Creed-Recitation on the Power of Belief."

Creed-recitation calms the conscious mind and permits the Unconscious to operate more fully. This is a psychologically sound principle as well as a mystical truth. Saints and hermits of old knew very well about the belief-provoking powers of creeds. Today we need a new knowledge of this truth, particularly since traditional and customary values are being challenged daily. For many the old ways have lost their meaning, their guiding capacity, and their efficacy. More and more theologians and philosophers are trying to help the people who are lost in the process.

Dr. Arthur M. Ramsey, the Archbishop of Canterbury, recently gave addresses at Oxford and Cambridge, which were published as *Introducing the Christian Faith*. Dr. Ramsey's words shed some light on what I mean when I say that the language of the Apostles' Creed can be altered to suit one's needs. Dr. Ramsey writes:

> There needs to be a greater acknowledgement of the poetical character of much religious language, with more frank explanation . . . There is a need to try to show that much about which the Christian faith speaks is happening within the experience of ordinary people, and that the Christian language focuses and interprets what is theirs already rather than assaults them with some sort of hobby or technicality from without.

HE SAID: "I WAS RAISED ON SCIENCE, NOT RELIGION."

I quoted the above statement by Dr. Ramsey at a seminar in Massachusetts recently and a young man named Bill N. argued against the validity of the doctor's premise. Bill readily admitted that he felt an inner source of strength, but that he could not relate it to religion or spiritual experience. Bill was a psychology major in college. His parents were science-oriented people, non-religious, but not irreligious. Bill felt very strongly that Dr. Carl Jung is the key to our society's religious and moral dilemmas. I had heard this before and related to what Bill was saying. I also had prepared a creed for such young people, one which had worked wonders for other youngsters. I gave it to Bill and explained to him that if he used it regularly in meditation or in prayerful attitude it would activate his power of belief.

This creed, like the others, is a passage to higher forces. In psychological terms, this one puts you in touch with the Higher Self, that which lies beyond the ego. Rewording the Apostles' Creed, I developed this psychological and scientific one:

THE HIGHER SELF CREED THAT ENHANCES YOUR DAILY LIVING

I *believe* in the Unconscious the Limitless Expanse, Synthesizer of all opposites:

And in the Self its essential element: which is pre-existent, born of the Primordial: suffered under human repression, was denied, avoided, and ridiculed: it fell into disuse; under extreme pressure it emerged anew: it burst into consciousness, and expresses the aims of the Unconscious the Limitless Expanse: from thence it shall proceed to heal the dissociated and the bewildered.

I *believe* in the Self: Transcendental Guidance; the synthesis of opposites: the integration of personality: the complementation of the Unconscious: and in Wholeness imperative.

Amen.

When Sandra K., of Seattle, Washington, used this creed, it was my good fortune to see her change from a high-strung, nervous young lady into a rock of strength. She had been uncertain of herself, indecisive, doubtful, and highly susceptible to fits of depression. After three weeks of reciting and intoning the Higher Self Creed she came back to the lectures I was giving. She was vivacious, confident, ready to survive any setbacks life might produce. Many other people have used this creed to fill their lives with new meaning, vital energy, and personal possessions. You will do the same if you apply yourself when reaffirming your own power of belief.

HOW CREEDS CAN MAKE THE GOOD BETTER AND THE BETTER BEST

Stanley F., of Atlanta, Georgia, had this to write after learning of the above-mentioned three creeds:

Dear Mr. Laurence:

I didn't get a chance to speak with you after the lectures at Simmony Hall, so I thought I'd write you a letter. I wanted to thank you for your enlightening and helpful series of lectures.

Until I heard you speak about creeds I was afraid to utter prayers other than the traditional ones, even though I must admit that I have failed to have my prayers answered. Some of my friends used to ridicule me because I wouldn't break off from my religion. I'm a Catholic. I want you to know that I respect the way you let another guy's religion alone and simply suggest that we try other creeds for activating our power of belief.

I have been using the Universal Mind Creed and the Higher Self Creed, as well as the Apostles' Creed, and I can only say that since I have been doing so I feel charged, or something. I'm not afraid to ask for anything from life. In fact, I just bought a new Pontiac, and that's something!

Thanks again. Hope to see you when you speak here next year.

Sincerely yours,
Stanley F.

Stanley wrote again about two months later. This time he wanted to tell me that his life in general had improved greatly. Two weeks later I heard from him again, a very enthusiastic note. He wrote: "I wanted things to get better, but I never dreamed 'better' could become 'best!' "

Stanley had learned well the lesson I was trying to teach: if you recite, intone, or chant these creeds, your power of belief expands and reflects in your daily life. It is because of this miraculous process that I have brought together a series of creeds for your edification.

I have seen these creeds work wonders in the lives of many people—businessmen and businesswomen, homemakers, laborers, factory workers, office clerks, janitors, and many more—and they can work wonders in your life if you activate your dormant power of belief.

Just how to use the creeds and just how they evoke your power of belief and put it to work is fully explained in subsequent chapters. Each chapter contains a single creed, set apart so you can study it, reflect upon it, and perhaps even memorize it.

Awaken your power of belief and it will work for you and fill your life with whatever you want. *Expect* your power of belief to create miracles. As Dr. Sockman puts it: "Expectancy expands the receiving faculties." If you want anything—money, position, food, power, personality, health, possessions—then arouse your power of belief and *expect* it to work for you. You don't have to do anything except expect. What could be easier?

2

How the Joy Creed Can Invigorate and Strengthen You

I would now like to share with you the experiences of some people from different walks of life and from different parts of the country. These people have had problems that are prevalent today in our chaotic society. Economic pressures, rapid cultural changes, and personal troubles combined to make them anxious and depressed. Anxious and depressed people do not operate at their optimum level of efficiency. Such emotions enervate you, hold you back, cloud the brain, and make you listless. The people whom I have seen cured, helped, uplifted and generally reanimated all used the Joy Creed, which is as follows for your benefit:

THE CREED THAT DISPELS
ENERGY-SAPPING EMOTIONS

I *believe* in Joy the Transcendent Emotion, Foe to anxiety and depression:
   And in Happiness its foremost phenomena: which is destined

for all men, born of Self-regulation: thwarted by reason, was called utopian, unrealistic, and unattainable: it therefore eluded man; it manifested again to the sincere searcher: it is present again as the physical manifestation of spiritual Joy: as the Transcendent Emotion it shall brighten the lives of the asker and the seeker.

I *believe* in Happiness: the fullness of life; the reality of gladness: the reduction of sadness and misery: the experience of exhilaration: and in Joy undaunted.

Amen.

This particular creed, I have discovered through experience, is most apropos at this time in our history. People everywhere are experiencing life's inequities and they need something dynamic to help them. For many this creed is the answer. It aids them during times of stress and crisis and during times of financial pressures and joblessness. Those who have used the Joy Creed have reaffirmed their belief in Joy and Happiness for themselves. Believing, they have discovered, is essential to life, happiness and survival. Their personal experiences point up what Loyola University Professor of Psychology Eugene C. Kennedy says in his new book, *Believing:*

> The research of social scientists reveals believing as a perennial function that is essential for man's survival; without it he will collapse in the face of life's inequities.

Life's inequities are all around us. The newspapers are filled with accounts of them. People everywhere are beset by them. I know some of these unfortunate people, men and women who *needed* to reaffirm and reactivate their power of belief.

SHE SAID: "IT'S A JOYLESS AND LOVELESS WORLD."

I did not argue with Gail H., of Topeka, Kansas, when she aired her views about life. She was still young, in her early twenties, but a recent job lay-off left her sullen, worried, and lacking in hope for the future.

She had been one of the most dedicated secretaries in a large aircraft company. She had worked harder for the company than any of the others. She had been secretary to a junior vice president, a member of a local Women's Liberation group, active in charitable organizations, and for three years a political activist, and she had marched in more demonstrations for the rights of others than anyone I've ever known.

And at every opportunity, Gail would speak publicly about life's inequities to groups of admiring listeners. When others dropped away, she did not. And when public interest waned, she clung to her principles, confident that if enough people spoke out, radical changes in social conditions would ensue.

Now, confronted by personal difficulties, she spoke to me despairingly as I sat in my office.

"I can't believe this," she said. "What do you think of recent developments in this country? I swear, when I look around at what's happening, I begin to have doubts about brotherly love. More and more good people are being laid off, prices are soaring, rents are fantastic. I thought that by being free and independent, I could make it in this dog-eat-dog society. Things have even gone better with the sweet Suzy-homemakers who let their hubbies do the worrying than they have with me. When I lost this super job my whole world collapsed. I didn't know I could be so negative, so low, but this thing has really got me down. What can I do?"

It was a good question. I could have shown her my records, many of which contain the same question asked by people all over the country, for many people are suffering dilemmas just like hers. The jobless and the employed are on equal footing here: how does one cope with rising costs? How does one deal with what often looks like social injustice? What can one do when life in general looks dismal and every day a drudgery?

HOW THE JOY CREED CAME INTO BEING

I could easily have turned Gail's problem over to a sociologist or a minister or a psychologist. Or I could have gotten into a long discussion with her about the trends of history, beginning with the cyclical rise and fall of economies throughout the world, and the state of our own economy with "the bottom dropped out." I could even have chastised her for her dark outlook and reminded her that she was actually better off than many others I know.

But none of that would have helped her. No, if I was going to be effective, I could reply in only one way.

I said, "I empathize with you, Gail. A hard-working, dedicated person like you should have gotten more for her efforts. You should be enjoying life. You're young, beautiful and vivacious. Life should be beckoning to you, not turning you away. I know how you feel and why you are depressed. You feel lost, tired, perhaps even used up. You are looking on the dark side of things at the present, letting outer conditions dictate your inner conditions."

Gail's blue eyes sparkled with interest. She was trying to understand me.

I asked her: "What do you think we should do? Should we gorge ourselves on all the negative conditions and circumstances which surround us today? Or should we somehow envision our own hopes and expectations, knowing that what we believe will come to pass? You have been looking in the wrong direction. You have been so active in the community, in the world, so to speak, that you are identifying with external circumstances and letting them guide your inner life. You are an energetic young woman, capable and efficient, but you've lost touch with your own power of belief. You have let outer conditions undermine your personal power. You have been believing that the world is coming apart—so *you* are! What we believe we become. What you think, you are!"

As I spoke with Gail, I was thinking about the creeds. The Apostles' Creed wouldn't suffice in this case. Nor would the Universal Mind Creed or the Higher Self Creed. Gail's problem weighed heavily on me, for it combined with others of similar nature. I remembered my files, reams of records containing other peoples' woes, trials and setbacks. I have known many Gails, male and female, men and women trying to cope in this sometimes overwhelmingly oppressive life. And as I sat with Gail the creeds took a new turn in my mind. And in an instant of intuition I knew how I could help Gail help herself. In those moments the seeds of the dynamic creeds which fill this book were planted. For Gail I developed the Joy Creed. It worked miracles in her life. It worked so well that I had hundreds of copies made up and mailed them to every person in my files who had problems similar to Gail's.

HOW THE JOY CREED CAN ENRICH YOUR DAILY LIFE

I explained to Gail that Joy is a spiritual quality and that what humans call Happiness is its physical manifestation. You have to *believe* in both in order to enjoy either.

Gail affirmed daily: "I *believe* in Happiness: the fullness of life; the reality of gladness: the reduction of sadness and misery: the experience of exhilaration: and in Joy undaunted. *Amen.*"

When I next saw Gail she was a different person, even more vivacious and enthusiastic than before she had been laid off from her good job. She entered my office beaming, blue eyes twinkling, white teeth flashing constantly. She was bubbling over with news for me, and sitting across from my desk, her words poured out in such a torrent that I had all I could do to keep up with her.

"It's remarkable!" she cried. "What a burden you lifted from my shoulders. It's almost like I had been blind or something. I can see! I started saying the Joy Creed that very night I left here and I've practiced it every single night for the past two weeks. Just look at this!''

Gail pushed a letter across the desk to me. It was from a radio station in Los Angeles, saying that the management had heard of her not only through the place of her last employment but also through interested parties who had heard her speak publicly. The radio station was offering Gail a position as moderator on a talk show. The starting salary was $500 per week.

I shared in Gail's joy and gladness, expressing my congratulations and my sincere good wishes for her bright future. But Gail wasn't finished. She laughed excitedly and said, "Look at the date on the letter!''

I did so, but the meaning was lost to me. Gail explained eagerly: "That's the day I started reciting the Joy Creed! Don't you see what that means? The very day I started affirming my belief that radio station was writing me a letter, offering me a fantastic job!''

Gail and I got into a discussion about cause and effect then. She was bright and intelligent; her mind sharp and penetrating. This was the surest sign that the creed had worked wonders in her life. She departed from my office a young woman with proper hope, and she promised to write me from Los Angeles.

I want to share her first letter with you because it indicates he validity of Gail's surmise about synchronicity. The letter arrived about a month and a half after I knew she had moved to the West Coast. The first portion informed me of her new life and the difficulty she had in settling down due to her excitement. The talk show, she said, was a powerful vehicle for reaching others, and she was in her glory. The next part of the letter had this to say:

> Remember that I pointed out the date of my letter from the radio station? Remember how I said it coincided with the first day of my creed recitation? Well, that was no accident. I'm convinced now that there is a direct relationship between saying

the creed with feeling and simultaneous events. The following chain of events will clarify what I mean:

On the night of the 24th I intoned the Joy Creed in a very prayerful attitude before going to sleep. The next day my boss gave me a check for $500 and said it was an advance to help me out because he knew that "settling down costs money." The check was dated the 24th! He told me he decided to give it to me the night before. He had been lying in bed thinking about me. I asked him if he remembered the time. He said about eleven. That's when I was praying the Joy Creed!

But that's not all. I started saying the creed mentally, during the day, on the 25th. This was my first day as moderator of the show. It was a total success!

On the 26th I was repeating the creed in my head as I worked on the day's script. Mr. R., my boss, came by the apartment and he helped me with it. That afternoon, the president of a bank attended the taping and he applauded!

Mr. R. helped me again on the morning of the 27th. We had coffee and donuts at a local restaurant, and I learned a lot about him. He's divorced and has an eight-year-old girl. He showed me a photo of her. She's an angel! The show was a hit.

On the evening of the 28th Bill—that's Mr. R.—took me to a play and dinner. He discusses everything with me—politics, religion, science, Women's Liberation—he's very intelligent and he respects my mind.

I could go on and on like this, Mr. Laurence, but I don't want to write you a book. To make a long story short, after about nine days of saying and thinking the Joy Creed, I had been in Bill's company hundreds of times (so it seems).

On the 3rd he asked for my views about divorced men with children. I just know he's going to ask me to marry him. And I'm going to say yes! I'm not going to be a "sweet Suzy-home-maker" but I'm sure going to be his wife!

Gail's letter continued in this vein for some length, every line lifting my heart and tickling my fancy. It was joyous news and a powerful testimonial in tribute to the efficacy of the Joy Creed. In fact, Gail was so overjoyed that she signed her letter: "A true *believer!*"

HOW THE JOY CREED BRINGS RICHES
AND POSSESSIONS

I mentioned earlier that the Joy Creed was so miraculously effective in the life of Gail that I mailed copies of it to others I knew who
needed help. How the Joy Creed worked wonders in their lives
clearly demonstrates how it can become a potent force in your life.
When you activate your power of belief, you make *more* possible the
attainment of goals, the achievement of tasks and the acquisition of
the good things in life.

HE BELIEVED THAT $10,000 WOULD
MAKE HIM MOST HAPPY

Phil A., of Scranton, Pennsylvania, was one of the needy people I
had in mind when I mailed out the Joy Creed. Phil had been the
owner-operator of a small grocery store. Rising costs and increased
living expenses had forced him out of business. He is the father of
three children. His wife cannot work. Phil grew despondent, for he
had put his "life's blood" into the small business. He wrote me, and
stated, "Just $10,000 would make me the happiest man alive. With a
chunk of dough like that I could save my business before all the stock
is gone. I could get back on my feet."

When Phil received the Joy Creed, he began using it immediately.
Both he and his wife recited it orally and mentally on a daily basis,
with feeling and expectation. Bill said he constantly kept the figure of
$10,000 clearly in mind. He and his wife were using the creed for
three days, awaiting word from various agencies around the state,
agencies they had written to for help. On the fourth day still no saving
word had arrived, but quite unexpectedly, a man came to visit Phil at
his home. The man was a bankrupt shoe store owner. He had a
proposition for Phil. He suggested: "Why don't we combine our
business skills and work together? I don't want to go into business by

myself again. Not now. We can go into partnership and I think we can make a go of it."

Phil reported that the man offered some money of his own with which to begin this new venture in Phil's store. How much money? Exactly $10,000!

"Phil's Grocery Store" is now "Phil and Ed's Breadbasket," and the business is solvent.

HOW A HOUSEWIFE GOT HER NEW HOME IN THE MIDDLE OF A FINANCIAL CRISIS

Mrs. Anthony P., of Wheeling, West Virginia, was a victim of oppressing and depressing social issues. The daily newspapers, filled with the negative aspects of our times, bombarded her mind and spirit. She despaired of getting the new home her husband had promised her. She doubted that business would be good enough to increase his income. Everywhere she looked and read, people were cutting back, doing without, some were even starving. How could she dare hope for a new home? The Joy Creed helped her overcome her less than desirable attitudes. It gave her a new hope for Happiness, which is the physical manifestation of Joy. She ceased looking at limitation and impoverishment and began seeing the reality of gladness, accomplishment and achievement. She reaffirmed her belief in the fullness of life, and her husband's income *did* increase. Mrs. P. now lives in her new suburban home in Wheeling; the home she was promised; the home she wanted more than anything else —even though its price had been raised to $34,989!

HOW THE JOY CREED TURNS YOUR ILLUSIONS AND EXPECTATIONS INTO REAL WEALTH

Sceptics are famous for ridiculing the believer. People who look forward to brighter futures and the acquisition of their needs and desires are often belittled. "Illusions, illusions!" cry the sceptics.

It's true! Positive-thinking people *do* have illusions. They have illusions of peace and plenty, joy and happiness, fulfillment and satisfaction. Such illusionists are the very heart of humanity! A man who ought to know is Rene Dubos, the eminent scientist and caring humanist. In his book, *A God Within,* Dr. Dubos says: "To assert that there is hope when everything looks so dark may appear a naive and pretentious illusion, but it is the kind of illusion that generates the creative faith of which Carl Sandburg wrote:

> I am credulous about the destiny of man,
> And I believe more than I can ever prove
> Of the future of the human race
> And the importance of illusions,
> The value of great expectations.

It is often difficult to retain faith in the destiny of man, but it is certainly a coward's attitude to despair of events."

Perhaps you have some strange illusions and far-fetched expectations. If you do, don't give them up! Illusions and expectations can be realized! With the activation and employment of the power of belief *any* hope can be materialized, lived, enjoyed and shared!

3

How the Truth Creed Puts You in Touch with the Source of Abundance and Plenty

In an ultra-rational, highly technological society, the power of simple belief is destroyed. A simple act of faith is replaced by intricate and complex thinking procedures. Power is lost to humans. In an age of violence and corruption, people forget how to believe. Torn from their roots that reach into the deeper layers of consciousness, people look more and more outside themselves for the answers to their troubles and dilemmas. We become severed from Truth.

Some people, after failure and heartbreak, come back to the roots. They ask for help and seek for the lost roots. They often find what they are looking for, and benefit thereby.

HOW WILLIAM R. BECAME A SINGING
SENSATION OVERNIGHT

William R. worked in a factory in Toledo, Ohio. It was a terrible job, he told me. "A crummy job. Bad lighting, poor pay and heavy

38

work. I work in steel, heavy stuff. I sweat all day. The power presses pound all day long and I come home with headaches. I make $2.25 an hour. I have to work a lot of overtime just to make ends meet—and those are pretty weak ends!''

William was a depressed individual, like so many others I have worked with. I engaged him in a conversation about the power of belief. He reacted bitterly.

He said: ''What belief? Belief in what? This is what's griping me. What good would it do for me to work up hopes about anything? What would I get? A pay raise? Or a harder job at the factory? Who needs it? Belief! Look around us! The rich get richer and the poor get ripped off! I was just reading in the paper the other day that even Ph. D.'s are getting laid off! What can I hope to advance to?''

I didn't permit William's negativity or bitterness to interfere with the purpose of our interview. He had come for practical help. I persevered and reminded him that each of us has an inner reservoir of strength and hope, that beyond our senses lies a vast storehouse of riches and happiness, if we can but get back in touch with it.

William scoffed at this reference to inner power, but he did not repudiate it. That was a good sign. I knew I could work with him. Even though he said, ''Science and technology have replaced faith and supernatural events,'' I taught him the Truth Creed. I shared the insightful words of Dr. Sockman with him: ''If we are to believe in ourselves, we must believe in the supernatural.''

I said, ''William, get a hold on yourself. Your very body is a physical manifestation of a spiritual entity. Get back to the roots of your faith. Activate your power of belief. Don't let external appearances fool you, delude you and misguide you. Sure, things are rough now. They'll get rougher if you continue to look outside yourself for help. The help you want and need lies within. When Jesus said, 'The kingdom of heaven is within,' he wasn't just uttering a platitude or a nice phrase. He was stating an unalterable fact of human life. I don't care how corrupt or evil the world looks to you. Inside there is Truth and Wisdom. Get in touch with that and you can do anything.''

William continued to think in terms of his factory job, limiting his potential for accomplishment. I told him to think further than that. To help him do this I inquired into his other skills, hobbies and talents. Through lengthy conversation I learned that he liked to sing, that during working hours, when the heavy machines are grinding and stamping and whirring, he sings his heart out. This interested me, for singing, like painting, writing, and playing music, are inner qualities and capabilities. This showed me that William did have contact with inner promptings. Singing, he said, made him feel happier even when things were at their worst.

All of this information tended to show that William could contact his own source of inner Truth and Wisdom. I taught him the Truth Creed. We recited it together a few times. I wrote it out for him. I made him promise to use it every night before falling asleep.

A week later William revisited my office. He sheepishly admitted that he had recited the creed with only half a heart. But, he added, he began to feel an inner stirring, a renewed sense of oneness with the flow of life. After the second night he began using the creed in earnest. Now, he told me, he was convinced that it was working for him.

How it ultimately worked for him is a joy to relate. Before two weeks were out, William no longer felt oppressed by outer circumstances. He had gotten in touch with his *inner* life, the life which precedes outer life.

One day, during a regular coffee break, William was at his machine. The factory had grown quieter as it does during such lulls in activity. William was still singing a song he had been singing over his machine. A hand touched his shoulder and he turned to see his boss standing next to him. His employer said, "I didn't know you could sing. That's a beautiful song. One of my wife's favorites."

William had been singing "My Wild Irish Rose," apparently very professionally. His boss and the man's wife were from Ireland. Put all of this together and you can guess what happened, but not quite. William's boss invited him to his home, to sing at a gathering of the town's upper class. William was a hit. His boss was so impressed that he took William aside and bluntly told him that he was fired. William was shocked until the man explained what he had in mind. He sent William to singing coaches, paid all of his expenses, bought him clothes for one-night stands, rented automobiles for his transportation. In short, the man spent thousands of dollars on William, and in what amounts to overnight, the greasy factory worker became an inspiring sensation.

William still writes every so often and mentions always that he continues to employ the Truth Creed to keep him in touch with the center within from which his singing talent emerges. And the state of the nation doesn't bother him in the least. He is enjoying prosperity, peace, plenty and satisfaction.

HOW THE TRUTH CREED CAN DO THE SAME FOR YOU

When you employ a verbal, faith-affirming device to get back to your roots (whether they are conscious or not) you tap an inner source of balancing, equalizing and steadying influences. The results of this tapping inner forces can result in any one of a number of things: riches, love, wisdom, psychic ability, healing, peace, strength and many more.

Others like William R. have used the Truth Creed to their ultimate joy and satisfaction. I find that those who use it most are people who find the present emphasis on intellect and reason alone inadequate to solve everyday problems. Needing something which would reactivate their power of belief and put them in touch with greater reality, they embraced the Truth Creed, and used it to their advantage.

Before I show you the creed which you can use at your leisure, here are some examples of those who have used it before you and have benefited from it.

HOW CHARLOTTE L. DISCOVERED THE
KEY TO INSTANT KNOWLEDGE

Charlotte L., of Pasadena, California, is a high school senior. She came to me with what she described as an insurmountable problem.

She was failing miserably in school and her father made it abundantly clear that if she did not come away with at least a B-average she would not receive the car he promised her; she would not go on summer vacation; she would not go out on dates and she would not have time for socializing with girlfriends because she would be too busy studying.

Charlotte was frustrated and worried. She always studied hard, she told me. Just in talking with her I could see that she was a highly intelligent girl. Too intelligent, I decided. She had no idea at all of the function of intuition, which is beyond intelligence.

I explained to Charlotte that intelligence is of the conscious part of the brain; intuition of the unconscious part. Thinking, I told her, can be forced, trained, controlled but intuition is a gift. It comes from within and has nothing to do with one's rational capabilities or powers of thought and reason.

The Truth Creed put Charlotte in touch with the center where intuitions are born and from which they emanate. She used the creed nightly for weeks. Her grades began to improve. She was startled to discover that sometimes she did not have to concentrate to come up with an answer to a problem in school. The mere question seemed to ring a bell within her and, as she described the process, "a door would open and there would be the solution. Just like that! It was stuff I'd read, but I don't have to think about the answer or squeeze it out of my memory. I just say the Truth Creed to myself and Poof! there's the answer!"

Did Charlotte achieve the required B-average? No. She graduated from high school a straight-A student!

HOW KEN S. OVERCAME INFERIORITY AND ACHIEVED SUCCESS

An overheard remark changed the entire course of Ken S.'s life. He was a janitor in an office building in Flagstaff, Arizona. One day as he was busily mopping the corridor, a group of well-dressed and important-looking businessmen passed by. One of them said, "You come up with some cost-cutting ideas or find yourself another job!"

Ken had heard many words that day, as he does every day, but these words plagued him for some reason. Ken was a steady user of the Truth Creed and that night as he recited it in bed, those words came back to him. Suddenly he had a series of short visions, strange visions. He saw the huge trash bins which sit outside the building. He saw stacks of stationery, desks, chairs and wall hangings. He saw typewriters.

Ken jumped out of bed, the experience was so uncanny to him. He didn't know what to make of it. Later, somewhat calmer, he returned to his bed and tried to sleep. But sleep would not come to him. Mentally reciting the Truth Creed didn't bring sleep; it brought mental activity and inner prodding. Suddenly, the strange visions took on meaning. Ken realized that he could provide that business-man with the ideas he needed! The mere thought of himself address-ing such a rich, professional person intimidated Ken, for he was shy and retiring. But the creed had put him in touch with his Higher Self, and the Self told him that he was not inferior, that he could and would obey this inner wisdom.

The following day found a bleary-eyed but confident Ken standing in the plush office of the president of a large industrial firm. He wrote and told me: "Even as I stood and talked away like I knew what I was saying, I was repeating the Truth Creed over and over in my head. The words just came tumbling out, clearly and intelligently. The man was impressed. He ordered a secretary to take down what I was saying about excessive waste, overstocking, overbuying of office equipment, and things like that. The more I said the creed, the more power flowed through me."

Ken is no longer a janitor. He's the purchasing agent for that firm—and he never went to college!

HOW THE TRUTH CREED CAN BRING
YOU ANYTHING YOU ASK FOR

There is nothing you cannot have if you know where to go to get it. No desire is too great, no wish too wild, no dream too fanciful and no hope too high, that it cannot be fulfilled by the inner source of power. The secret is to get to that source. As human beings, external-oriented beings, we require some system or avenue to that dynamic source of inspiration, wealth, and happiness. The Truth Creed serves exactly this purpose: a workable method for traveling inward, the link between conscious and unconscious worlds. When intellect, thinking, and reason don't help to bring into your life the things you want, then is the time to try to get inside to the very source of all things. Others have done it; so can you!

HOW THE TRUTH CREED DEVELOPED
HER PSYCHIC ABILITIES

Marion T., of Cincinnati, Ohio, wanted to develop her Tarot-card-reading ability. She used the Truth Creed to get back in touch with the inner source of knowledge, and ultimately developed an enlightening synthesis of astrology and the Tarot.

HOW THE TRUTH CREED SAVED A GIRL FROM SUICIDE

A distraught mother begged me to visit her young daughter who was interned in a mental institution. I did so, only to discover that eighteen-year-old Heather P. was not suffering from any mental disease, but was a victim of great depression. Her psychiatrist talked with me for a few moments and said that Heather's main problem was that she had lost the will to live. Heather had tried to commit suicide. I sat with her on a sun porch for some twenty or thirty minutes. She was listless and negative, but happy to have a visitor. She didn't think she belonged in this place. I agreed with her, and told her that she and only she would be the key to freedom. I provided her with the Truth Creed and she promised to try to use it.

Heather was released a few weeks later, after doctors were assured that her unexpected buoyancy wasn't a temporary manic state. Her psychiatrist informed me that he felt Heather's reawakened power of belief in life saved her from death or from a fate worse than death. Heather uses the Truth Creed to this day and is living a full and happy life in Chicago, Illinois.

THE TRUTH CREED THAT WORKS WONDERS

Here now is the Truth Creed, the same one the above people used to recharge their lives with meaning and purpose. You can use it at your leisure, at work, at play, in the home and in the office. Mentally or orally, the Truth Creed is a point of contact between your outer circumstances and your innermost life-force.

I *believe* in Truth the Foundation of Life, Adversary to ignorance and prideful intelligence:

And in Wisdom its gift to mankind: which is basic to life, basic to love: subverted by intellect, was devalued, displaced, and defamed: it ceased to guide man; in an age of violence and corruption it re-emerged: it sounded a clarion call, and infuses with knowledge all who reaffirm Truth as the Foundation of Life: ultimately to enlighten the lowly and the meek.

I *believe* in Wisdom: unconscious knowledge; the superiority of the Self: its capacity to confer knowledge: the limitations of reason alone: and in Truth unfathomable.

Amen.

4

How the Good Fortune Creed Changes Your Luck for the Better

A few weeks ago I had an interview with a young man who was terribly depressed because "things were against him." He said that after five years of lack and impoverishment he was ready to throw in the towel. His luck, he said, was worse than rotten. I explained to him the meaning of Good Luck. Luck is not mere chance, hit-or-miss events, as many people believe. Rather it is a *force;* a latent, potent force resident in your unconscious. The power of belief reaches this force and starts it flowing in your own life. All you have to do is *believe* that there is a steady flow of good luck within you: *believe* and receive!

I advised this young man to dispense with all of his preconceptions about what luck is. I also suggested that he ignore the world's definition of luck. Luck is the physical manifestation of Transpersonal Goodness. To put him in touch with this inner storehouse of good fortune, I gave this man the Good Fortune Creed, which has helped hundreds of others to reactivate their power of belief and thence to fill their lives with hope, blessings, the good things of life.

THE CREED THAT TRANSFORMS ILL FATE INTO GOOD FORTUNE

I *believe* in Good Fortune the Sign of Blessing, Opponent to ill fate and bad luck:

And in Good Luck its physical manifestation: which man once understood as divine blessing, born of belief: disavowed by modern rationalism, was degraded, disregarded, and disparaged: it was rendered impotent; called superstitition by the masses, it lay dormant: it exists only for believers, and waxes effective for those who know Good Fortune as the Sign of Blessing: for them it shall materialize in home and in business.

I *believe* in Good Luck: help from on high; the influence from the Self: Transcendent Goodness: the source of blessings: and in Good Fortune immeasurable.

Amen.

HE SAID: "THAT CREED HAS GIVEN ME THE MIDAS TOUCH!"

The young man mentioned above used this creed faithfully. He affirmed his own power of belief, and in using the creed, he re-established his link with the source of all good fortune.

He said to me, "I know now what the power of belief can do: it can give you the Midas touch!" This young man realized that no matter what outer conditions look like, inner resources can change them. The point to remember is this: Good Fortune is always seeking to manifest itself through you. Activate your power of belief; recite the Good Fortune Creed and let your unconscious know that you believe. Then expect wonderful and exciting changes in your life.

So many wonderful things began to happen to the young man above that he was astounded. He got a better-paying job without even looking for it! His new employer sought *him* out! He met a new woman who now brightens his life. The new car he has been deprived of for years is now his. Things like this continue to happen for him, and he remarks: "It's uncanny. It's like it doesn't matter what I do: it turns into gold!" Even seeming setbacks have worked to his good. He has become like the man in the old Arab proverb which says: "Throw a lucky man into the sea and he will come up with a fish in his mouth."

HOW THE GOOD FORTUNE CREED GAVE HER A NEW LIFE

Not very long ago, during a stay in Boston, Massachusetts, I had a long conversation with a woman named Cheryl B., who told me that her loveless marriage was "souring life" for her. This young woman, only twenty-four years old, had a burden of heartaches that even older women don't accumulate. Her husband had been cheating on her for at least two years and she had quietly and tacitly accepted this behavior, because she was "afraid of losing him." He treated her shabbily, bought her few clothes, rarely took her out, but at the same time, expected her to take care of the house, clean, do his laundry, and look presentable when he brought clients and fellow employees home to dinner.

She said, "I don't think I've been happy in years."

I explained to this poor soul that the things she wanted and needed out of life, the love, the security and the fullness of living, do not lie within the range of her husband's powers. The fundamental, enriching power she was seeking lies within, in the unconscious. The Self alone is able to provide for human needs and wants. All you have to do is permit it to express itself. "Let go and let God," as the saying goes.

Following my explanation that her husband is but one symbol of her own inner lack and inadequacy, Cheryl turned to the Unconscious. Using the Higher Self Creed to reactivate her power of belief, she affirmed:

I *believe* in the Self: Transcendental Guidance; the synthesis of opposites: the integration of personality: the complementation of the Unconscious: and in Wholeness imperative.
Amen.

This exercise in getting to know herself helped Cheryl to understand and rely upon the latter part of the Good Fortune Creed:

I *believe* in Good Luck: help from on high; the influence from the Self: Transcendent Goodness: the source of blessings: and in Good Fortune immeasurable.
Amen.

In just a matter of weeks great changes began to take place in Cheryl's life. First she witnessed a change in her own mental attitude. She began to understand that many of her husband's faults were also her own, the kind she didn't want to admit to herself. It was easier to see them in her husband.

In time, her husband noticed this basic change in her. He couldn't put his finger on it, but he was certain that something was happening to his wife. I interviewed Bill as part of my post-counseling operation.

He said, "Cheryl started getting independent. All of a sudden she stopped leaning so heavily on me, like a little girl incapable of caring for herself. One day I came home from work to find her typing. Cheryl hadn't touched a typewriter since high school. I asked her what she was doing and she said she was brushing up. The next thing I knew she was talking about going to work, getting out of the house. She got a job as a typist in a local company. She shares the expenses of living with me. She thinks for herself. As far as I'm concerned, Cheryl is a new woman. And a lovely one. When I saw her in her work clothes I thought I was seeing a different person. She was beautiful, radiant, attractive. I had been used to seeing her in house-dresses, dragging her heels. Our whole love life is renewed, fresh, exciting. It's a miracle!''

Cheryl solved her personal problems after realizing that Good Fortune does not come from someone else, but from within. This demonstrates to all of us that, yes, we need a mate, a home, a car, money, love, security, and some fun, but more, we need to get in touch with the *source* of all these things, the *true* source, the Higher Self, the Unconscious. Even our consciousness is a product of the Unconscious. We need reason, intelligence, will, yes, but these emerge from within. As the religious person would put it, all that is comes from God.

BEGIN TO CHANGE YOUR LUCK NOW

Before going to sleep, meditate on the creed of your choice. Some of my friends concentrate on all of them. In your mind's eye, look at the problem challenging you. Review your circumstances, the conditions of your life. If you think you are having ''bad luck'' you can have it changed *for* you. Not through mind power or ego control or sheer power of will, but by letting go and permiting the Higher Self to become real and active in your realm of existence. You will soon discover that, no matter how bad your luck may be, a whole new world is available to you. *Expect* change!

FIND OUT HOW GOOD LUCK MATERIALIZES

Greg D., of Springfield, Illinois, is a lawyer who has senatorial aspirations. He is just out of law school and he is young and inexperienced at this time. He recognizes this fact, but he doesn't let it bother him. Greg is trusting in his Higher Self, the source of Good Fortune. He openly states that the political scene is a dubious one. There is no certainty that he will succeed, not if he depends on outer conditions and circumstances. Greg does not depend on these things. He points out that he recognizes fully that there are forces yet unknown to man, higher forces, guiding forces that can and will aid humanity if humans will permit it. Greg realizes that luck has to be with him and that an awful lot of things depend on luck in the political arena. He has made it a habit to turn inward to the Transcendent Fount of all blessings within himself by affirming: "I *believe* . . ."

YOU HAVE THE KEY TO GOOD LUCK

The key to Good Luck is your ability to turn to the Unconscious, the Self. That key is in your hands. No one can force you to turn. *You* have to do that. But that's *all* you have to do. Choose one or more creeds, recite them with feeling, turn inside, and the worst of luck can be transformed, altered, changed and improved. Miracles and wonders can occur in your life when you turn the key you alone possess.

Look well into thyself; there is a source which will always spring up if thou wilt always search there.
—Marcus Antoninus

Doubt whom you will, but never yourself. (your Self)
—Bovee

I have ever held it as a maxim never to do that through another which it was possible for me to execute myself.
—Montesquieu

For they can conquer who believe they can.
—Vergil

HOW THE GOOD FORTUNE CREED CAN
MAKE LIFE EASIER FOR YOU

Believe in the outer way, and you must toil by the sweat of your brow for the things you want; believe in the inner way, and the things of life come *to* you, and toil itself is transformed into pleasure. Does this sound miraculous? Think about it. When you are cut off from the inner source of All, you must labor, strive, suffer, and wish, then taking what life gives you.

Frequent affirmation of your power of belief, trust in higher-than-human agencies, will work wonders for you. The choice is yours whether you are going to work and slave for a thing or open your heart and simply receive it. Believe and receive. As Jungian analyst Frances G. Wickes puts it in her superb book, *The Inner World of Choice:* "The inward choice of the transforming power of the spirit flows into the daily act." In other words, as you think, so you are; as you believe, so you receive. Affirm the influence of the Self and it will manifest in your outer life. The main difference between the ego-controlled individual and the Self-controlled person is that the former must strive and manipulate life in order to obtain what he wants, while the latter simply evokes his own power of belief and lets things come to him.

George F. owns a new convertible. Alex M. also owns a new convertible. Outwardly they seem alike in this respect. But they are worlds apart and very different. George is working hard, often overtime, to meet the payments on his car. More than once he has been threatened with repossession, which scared him to death. He works harder and harder to get enough money to keep those payments up. On the other hand, Alex is a man who turned to the Self months ago and practices the creeds regularly, permitting life to happen *to* him. Alex won his convertible, free and clear, in a sweepstakes contest which was held by a leading soap manufacturer.

Margaret N., of Peoria, Illinois, lost her job as a secretary to a more qualified person. Although she would rather write novels, she attended night school for more than a year to improve her condition in life. She succeeded. But Barbara L., of the same city, who always liked dabbling in the mystical and the occult, turned to the Self, and now she is a highly intuitive fortune teller, who charges $10 per reading. She clears about $50 a day, and that means $250 per week!

These are just examples of the differences among people. It does not mean that you should not go to school to better yourself. But it does mean that when you turn to the source of all Good Fortune and affirm your power of belief, miracles can occur in your life without your having lifted a finger!

Others are doing it, so can you! Change luck to suit you. Alter your circumstances. Help the Higher Self to help you by affirming your power of belief.

Affirm, "I *believe* in Good Luck: help from on high; the influence from the Self . . ." and *expect,* look forward to, anticipate wonderful, life-changing events to appear.

5

How the Love Creed Makes Others Help You, Support You, and Sustain You

The following is a portion of a taped interview with one of my New York clients, used here with his permission. It speaks for itself and serves as an excellent illustration of how the Love Creed can enhance your life.

> After having heard a series of your talks on Love, I realized that I've come a long way from the feelings of charity and brotherly love I had learned in childhood. My mother had been very careful to teach us children the worth of loving our neighbors. I had gotten out of touch with those maternal teachings. Life had gotten in the way. The more I listened to you, the more I could see that I've let certain social issues and conditions to color my thinking and feeling. Here I am, almost forty years old, and it took a week of lectures to break through my tough exterior.

I've been reciting the Love Creed every night before falling to sleep. It has changed my whole life. I feel friendlier towards others. People interest me for the first time in years. I'm beginning to look on the positive side of human nature, not letting negative reports cloud my thinking. I've gained a strong sense of unity again. I've stopped separating people into categories in my head: the rich and the poor, the strong and weak, the superior and inferior.

In this day and age of cut-throat behavior and devisive beliefs, the Love Creed reminds me of my initial love for all of humanity. I think we need more of that kind of love today.

THE LOVE CREED THAT TEARS DOWN WALLS THAT SEPARATE YOU FROM HAPPINESS

This is the Love Creed that my New York friend and many other clients are using:

I *believe* in Love the Essence of Life, Unifier of man and woman:

And in Brotherhood its chief expression: which is formed by Higher Guidance, born of the full Heart: suffered under worldly conditions, was suppressed, ignored, and forgotten: it declined into oblivion; in troubled times it rose again from the depths: it experienced a rebirth, and manifests as the true expression of Love the Essence of Life: from thence to unite the strong and the weak.

I *believe* in Higher Guidance: the Brotherhood of Humanity; the equality of all people: the correction of lovelessness: the elevation of human spirit: and in Love eternal.

Amen.

This is the creed that can make you glad to be alive. With practice it can become *your* creed. Once it is active in your Unconscious, it will reflect in your outer life. People will interest you, help you, like you, want to be near you. This creed makes all people *human beings*, not statistics, numbers, or puppets.

HOW THE LOVE CREED SAVED A MAN
AN ESTIMATED $1380

Bert S., of Boulder, Colorado, shared his remarkable experience with me when I returned to that city for a seminar. Bert had been using the Love Creed since my last visit, which was some four months earlier.

He said, "I've got to tell you how this creed worked for me. Now, I've been a guy set in his ways for almost thirty years. I thought I had things pretty well figured out—until I attended your lectures and started using that Love Creed. It happened like this: I had been saving up some things over the years, buying when I could, storing them for the day when I could afford to renovate my home. Well, as you know, prices have soared. Labor is expensive. Here I was prepared to get the house fixed up but I was stopped dead by the prices being asked for work done. That was one problem. My other problem was that I've been a stiffnecked, old codger. I go to church every Sunday and I always thought I loved my neighbors, like the good book says. But across the street from my place, some young people moved in, about six or seven of them, male and female. Now I didn't like that. It was easy for me to love my neighbor when I was thinking of Mrs. T. next door, or Mr. V. or old Sam N. But not those Hippies. No, sir, I just couldn't think of them as neighbors. I'd heard too many reports about people like them. But, do you know what happened? It was those very people who came to my aid when I needed help most."

Bert explained this remark by showing me his estimate for fixing up his home. The list he showed me read:

House Painting ....$ 800
Carpentry ....$ 80
Furniture Refinishing ....$ 200
Landscaping ....$ 300
Total $1380

The magic happened, he told me, when he started practicing the Love Creek, when he reawakened his dormant love of humanity and allowed his power of belief in his fellow man to take hold of him.

One day, after a long night of soul-searching and recitation of the Love Creed, Bert made up his mind to make friends with his new neighbors, to swallow his prejudice, to de-program himself. He went across the street and introduced himself. The long-haired youths were delighted to see him. He was the first neighbor to show a sign of friendliness. The group of youths were ecstatic. Bert had tea with them, got into conversations with them, even invited them over to his house for an evening of chess and coffee. Just in passing conversation, Bert mentioned his problem concerning the cost of fixing his home. The response from the young people was instantaneous and altruistic.

Bert said, "One of them was a genuine carpenter! Another had painted lots of houses. A girl was great at landscaping property. She was a college graduate! Another boy knew how to work with furniture. His father had been a cabinet-maker. And another one said he could put my sink in with no trouble.

"When I asked them how much all this would cost, they laughed and said, 'Nothing!' I couldn't believe it. I thought they were pulling my leg, but they assured me that they meant it. They said they loved to work and that they could 'really get into' fixing up my house.

"And they did! And I've never seen a more professional job anywhere. They came by every day, laughing and singing and playing musical instruments, and all the same, got the work done. I was so touched by the finished product that I almost cried. When I told a young girl that I just couldn't accept all of this for free, she smiled and said, 'Just love us.'

"I believe the Love Creed did all this for me. It opened my heart and my mind. The biggest lesson I learned from all of this is: you can't judge a book by its cover."

HOW THE LOVE CREED MAKES YOU
IMPORTANT TO OTHERS

Bert learned another lesson: people really want to love him. When you activate the power of Love which resides in the Unconscious, it brings new and loving people into your life and binds you to them and them to you. As the English philosopher Robert Burton has said: "No cord nor cable can so forcibly draw, or hold so fast, as love can do with a twined thread."

If Bert thought the young people were important in *his* life, it was nothing compared to how important he was to *them*. Rejected, despised, ridiculed, they found a true friend in this man from the older generation. The Love Creed had spanned the generation gap!

HOW A NEW YORK WOMAN ACHIEVED
PERSONAL FULFILLMENT

Marlene F., a New York City woman recently divorced, came to me in a highly emotional state. She was completely depressed and nervous, symptoms of her loss of faith in life. The divorce had shaken her very foundations and she felt all was lost. What hurt her the most was that she had loved her husband with all the love she could muster. I explained to Marlene that love cannot be centered around only one person to the exclusion of all others. Marlene needed renewed confidence in the power of love.

She started reciting the Love Creed nightly, opening up her closed channels to Universal Love. As she practiced the creed, more and more people were allowed into her life. Love, she discovered, was not lost simply because she had been divorced by an unfeeling man.

Marlene was revitalized. Life came back to her. She was reanimated. And personal love resulted. She met a man at a social gathering and she found that he could love as completely as she. They are married now and both of them use the Love Creed. They keep a copy of it in a frame over their bed. Lovelessness, for Marlene, was banished when she turned to Higher Guidance.

HOW A MAN CAME TO MARRY THE WOMAN HE DESPISED

Paul W., of Toronto, Canada, is an illustrative example of what can happen in your life when you permit the Self to act in your life. Paul was a militant enemy of Women's Liberation groups in general and of independent females in particular. He would not date any woman who expressed feminist views. The affirmation of the Love Creed re-established his psychic link with this outcast group of women. In his efforts to love humanity, he found that he had also to love liberated females. Because he was sincere and basically self-honest, he forced himself to attend some women's forums. The last time he wrote to me, he said, "I shudder to think that I could have gone on hating this kind of woman. If I hadn't opened to Higher Guidance and Brotherhood I would never have met Claudia!"

Claudia was the president of a chapter of a women's group. She is now Paul's wife—and she retains her title: Ms. E.

TO HAVE LOVE YOU HAVE TO BELIEVE IN LOVE

The Love Creed stimulates your dormant power of *belief* in love. Through affirmations like the Love Creed you tap unconscious resources, and the center of Universal Love. Your outer life then reflects this activation of inner love. The more you affirm the equality of all people, the Brotherhood of Humanity, and Love eternal, the greater are your chances of receiving love, friendship, companionship, and partnership.

The Higher Self, activated by your own power of belief in Love, sends out invisible rays, as it were, psychic feelers that make contact with people who can help you, and it draws these people to you to lighten your life. Through the use of the Love Creed you can attract friends, lovers, companions, helpmates and sponsors. This capacity is within everyone, but you will empower yours and make it more effective when you contact the inner world of power and energy. The Love Creed puts you in touch with that center.

6

How the Self-Confidence Creed Builds a Dynamic Personality

Dr. Ralph M. was among the eighty-three people who attended my lectures on the power of the Transpersonal in Louisville, Kentucky. During a consultation, he asked me: "What is self-confidence and why do I lack it?" As I talked with him I learned that although he had a flourishing practice, he himself lacked confidence when dealing with people in his personal life. I was surprised to learn that he had few friends, that his private life was dull and barren. During our discussion he revealed that he had spent hundreds of dollars on personality development courses. He had followed all the rules to the letter, he lamented, but his self-confidence just didn't grow.

I asked Dr. M. to write on a piece of paper the words: self-confidence. He did so and I looked at it. I was looking to see if he capitalized the word Self. He did not and that helped me to help him.

I explained to him that the Self is not *my*self, but *the* Self. When we speak of self-confidence, we mean *confidence in the Self*. The Self is Transpersonal, above and beyond physicality, transcendent to this dimension. The Self has been variously known as Universal Mind, God, Buddha and other deific appelations. That's a far cry from *my*self, unless we separate that word and render it correctly as my Self.

THE SECRET TO PERSONALITY, CHARACTER, AND CHARISMA

Dr. M. eventually learned that the power of personality he was seeking *outside* actually resides *within*. He got in touch with the Self, instead of *him*self, and *received*—not developed, worked up or willed—but *received* the confidence that was lacking in his life. His days and nights thereafter were filled with interesting and friendly people. His whole life was brightened. He gained assurance, respect, and character. The secret lies within you, in the unfathomed and unfathomable Unconscious. Once tapped, confidence wells up from within and overflows into your outer life. You become the *vehicle* for confidence.

HOW TO BECOME A LIVING CHANNEL OF ENERGY AND VITALITY

I explained to this lecture group that when you do not capitalize in your mind and heart words like self-confidence, self-respect, self-esteem, and so forth, you are referring not to the limitless and potent Higher Self, but to the limited and inflated Ego. Small lettered "selfs" and capital "I's" refer to Ego, that pompous and prideful element in each of us which would gladly prevent us from reaching the true Self. This is why the Bible records: "Not I but Christ in me." Christ, as Dr. Carl Jung amply points out, is a symbol of the Self. When the saint says, "Not I but Christ in me," he means not myself but my Self does the work. He is saying in effect, "I am but the channel for higher forces." This humble attitude, which by worldly standards is humiliating, charges the saint with power, energy, vitality, and personality.

You become a living channel of vigor, spirit, zest, magnetism, and charisma to the degree that you permit the Self, the Transcendent, to operate *through* you.

THEY WANTED TO BE MORE PERSONABLE, SUCCESSFUL, AND ADMIRED

The eighty-three people of Louisville, Kentucky were assembled together because they all wanted more out of life. They wanted greater confidence in themselves, a greater degree of personal charm, greater effectiveness in their daily lives.

Mona C. was suffering from an inferiority complex, and she wanted very badly to overcome it, to gain new and exciting friends and to be more personable herself.

Joe K. was a salesman, a door-to-door salesman, and he lamented that with the changing times it was getting more and more difficult to "reach" the consumer. He said: "You just can't hack it in this job unless you've got what it takes. I haven't got it. When a lady closes the door in my face, I feel defeated. How am I going to make a living if I feel like that?"

Barry L. had a personal problem. He wanted to meet the girl who waitressed at a local restaurant. When I asked him why he didn't just go up to her and introduce himself, he dropped his eyes and muttered, "I can't."

These are very human problems, but they need not be overwhelming ones. There is a way to overcome such debilitating difficulties. The Overcomer of these obstacles is the Higher Self. My client-friends got in touch with the Overcomer by using the Self-Confidence Creed, which is presented here for your edification:

THE CREED THAT OPENS THE DOOR TO
PERSONAL VITALITY

I *believe* in Self-Confidence the Impetus of Action, Enemy to fear and worry:

And in the Transpersonal its true source: which was once recognized, and tapped through introspection: distorted by ego-inflation, was reduced, personalized, and devitalized; it was supplanted by ego-control; in the Nuclear Age it reasserted itself: it waits for the humble, and responds to those who aspire to *true* Self-Confidence the Impetus of Action: to them it shall reveal the secrets to success and happiness.

I *believe* in the Transpersonal: the Infinite Unconscious; the Higher Self: the limitations of ego-consciousness: the Greater-than-I: and in Self-Confidence illimitable.

Amen

HOW SOME WALLFLOWERS TURNED INTO DYNAMOS

Anyone who has ever suffered stage fright, whether in school or later in public life, will appreciate the joy of Mona C. after she tapped her inner source of vital energy. Mona was delighted, enthusiastic and surprised at herself for when the inner power had started flowing through her, she found herself speaking before an audience, something she could never have done before. Having learned her lesson well, she put it to me in these terms: "I found my *Self* speaking before that audience. I let go. I mentally recited the last part of the Self-Confidence Creed over and over, even as the words came out of my mouth. The timid, frightened little me was no longer ascendant. The Self came through. I'm a new person!"

Joe K. *received* such an abundant supply of get-up-and-go that he graduated from selling inexpensive items door-to-door to demonstrating expensive machines for million-dollar companies. Timidity and defeatism had been giving him about $200 per week as a door-to-door salesman. Joe now tells me: "When I don't rake in at least a grand, it's a bad week."

Barry L.'s creed-recitations nightly brought him such an unlimited supply of energy and confidence, that he went overboard. He came to see me one day, beaming and delirious with happiness. He burst out that he had not only introduced himself to the waitress but had taken her out, wined, dined, and danced her. "Do I hear wedding bells?" I asked. Barry looked incredulous as though I had said something stupid. Then he chuckled, and said, "Diane's nice, but, no, no weddings for me. You see, there's this certain stewardess. . . ."

HOW THE POWER OF BELIEF ELECTRIFIES YOUR CREED-RECITATION

The Louisville group—and other groups across the country, I might add—learned how to tap their own inner resources—not the ego's, but the Self's—and they permitted that inexhaustible flow of energy to pass through them into their outer lives.

One young man asked: "Isn't that like annihilating my ego?" Not at all. Look at the Self-Confidence Creed again. When you say, "I *believe* in the Transpersonal: the Infinite Unconscious; the Higher Self, etc.," the "I" in the equation *is* the ego! You see, we are composite beings, made up of various elements. The ego is one, the Higher Self is another. It is the ego which says, "I *believe*." In other words you are training your dominant and sometimes interfering ego to be humble, to let go of the controls, to permit higher-than-human forces to enter your realm of being.

When the ego learns not to be so prideful and prejudiced, suprapersonal agencies can go to work in your life. When you affirm the "Greater-than-I" you are in effect asking God to enter your life; you are welcoming transcendent forces into your being. When this occurs in your particular life, self-confidence, dynamism, charm, magnetism, vitality, energy, power—all of these things and more are made available to you. But you must *believe* in the Self, the Transpersonal, the Greater-than-I. The ego believes something else entirely.

You see, the fact of the matter is that we are believing all the time.

We are believing in *something*. Joe K. believed that he was inferior, a defeatist. Mona C. believed she was inadequate, weak and unpersonable. Barry L. believed he could not address a strange woman. This negative use of the power of belief is as effective as the positive use of it. If you *believe* you can't, you never will.

I have talked of a prideful, dominating ego. It is wise to remember that the ego is also a weakling, and like many people who are weaklings, it boasts and brags and pretends to be strong. But it is the ego which quailed in Mona's life. It was Joe's ego that was timorous. Barry's ego was afraid to approach women. Underlying all of these personal problems was the seething, negative power of belief. You don't want to believe what the ego believes. Not if it is not productive, uplifting and saving. You want to believe in the Higher Self, in God, in the Transpersonal, the Greater-than-I. And the Self-Confidence Creed can help you rechannel your power of belief. Then, once your power of belief is positivized, it in turn electrifies your creed-recitation. The creeds become indispensable tools for you in your daily life to bring you the things you want, need and deserve.

HOW TO LET THE POWER OF BELIEF COME TO YOUR AID

Reactivate your power of belief in the good things of life by reciting the creed silently or audibly, whichever you choose, or both, *Know* that the Higher Self, the Greater-than-I *wants* to provide you with the energy and personal power you desire. Recite the creed daily or nightly before falling to sleep. If you know you are going to need powerful self-confidence for something tomorrow, next week, or next month, recite the Self-Confidence Creed with faith and intensity, and you will find that, even though the ego may quaver, the Self will imbue you with spontaneous and elevating confidence, personal power and sparkling character.

7

How the Health Creed Insures Your Own Wholeness and Vitality

There is a fundamental Karmic Law which was worded by the Master in this way: "Do unto others as you would have them do unto you." This law works on every level of human life, and when we put it into practice, we often find ourselves blessed. Simply stated: when you do good, good comes to you. When you wish others well, *you* are well. When you sympathize with the sufferings of others, your own suffering is minimized.

Life experience reveals again and again that truly healthy people (who *continue* to be healthy) possess one increasingly rare quality: the ability to empathize, feel for others, and to care about humanity.

What often escapes some people is that their own state of health is inextricably linked with the health of others. When I meet with a sick person I first find out his or her attitude toward others who are ill.

THE HEALING POWER OF EMPATHY

Three months ago I talked with a mine worker in West Virginia, a young man who had to quit working due to respiratory illness. Like others who had come down with various lung diseases, he attributed his illness to working in underground shafts. However, doctors assured him that his was not a dangerous disease, although they understood that he was nonetheless in great pain and severely limited in the things he could do in his condition. Since the doctors would not believe that he was "dying of lung cancer," as he put it, he resigned himself to dying. He actually believed that he was about to face death, and this debilitating belief was destroying the man. It was his distraught and worried wife who wrote to me and asked me to come see him.

I talked with Ben Y. for some time. He seemed genuinely glad to see me, but he was suffering from a particular delusion. From his sick bed, he said, "God, thank you for coming. Please help me. The doctors are all crazy. I'm dying. I don't want to die. Help me."

I said, "I can't help you. But you can help yourself. If you are willing to try to do that I'll do all I can."

Ben mistakenly thought that I had come to hold his hand while he died. He thought I would agree with his own diagnosis of his illness. And worse, he hoped that I would provide him with affirmations which would heal him miraculously. I did none of these things.

I said, "Ben, you're lying in bed when the best thing for you is to be up and about, exercising your body, getting sunshine and fresh air. You can talk. You can walk. Sure you cough and choke, but you have the use of more faculties than many of your co-workers. I've been to the local hospitals. Have you? Have you seen the condition some of your fellow workers are in?"

Ben admitted that he had never visited a hospital. "How can I?" he cried. "Look at me! I'm a mess!"

"You sure are!" I agreed. "You're a mess because you are wallowing in self-pity. Pity is meant for others, not for yourself. Now, if you really want to get well, take my advice and go visit the hospitals. See what you can do to help others who are sick. Then you will feel health infusing your own body."

Ben reluctantly took my advice and visited with a series of men laid up in hospital wards, men afflicted seriously with emphysema, bronchitis, cancer, and a host of other deadly diseases. When I saw Ben a few days later, he was greatly changed. He was humbler, quieter, less self-pitying.

He said: "You wouldn't believe the pain and suffering going on in those men. Some of them are being eaten away by horrible illnesses. It was a terrible experience for me, but I learned a lesson."

Ben did learn a valuable lesson, one which we all learn in this life if we are fortunate, a lesson best expressed in these words: "I cried because I had no shoes until I met the man who had no feet."

Once Ben had learned this most productive of human lessons I was able to provide him with the Health Creed.

THE HEALTH CREED THAT CREATES GOOD KARMA FOR YOU

I *believe* in Health the Condition of Wholeness, Healer of life and limb:

And in Empathy, its vital corollary: which is the mark of merciful humans, born of sympathy: fell prey to man's inhumanity to man, was neglected, withheld, and abused; it ceased to succor the ailing; in mankind's hour of need it reawakened: it embraced the suffering, and emanates from those who know Health the Condition of Wholeness: through them it shall manifest to help the sick and the halt.

I *believe* in Empathy: the caring for others; the health of fellow beings: their right to aid: the healing of affliction: and in Health unlimited.

Amen.

HOW TO KNOW THE SECRET TO HEALTHY
MIND, BODY, AND SOUL

A dedicated homemaker in Keene, New Hampshire once said to me: "I love taking care of my husband and children. I enjoy keeping house. And yet, I felt unfulfilled with my daily life. It grew so routine. I started getting listless, and that isn't healthy for any woman. When I started using the Health Creed, I got the idea to start a halfway house for runaway teenagers. I can't tell you how good it makes me feel in body, mind and soul when these kids tearfully thank me for helping them."

Here is a woman who, though she has a million things to take care of for herself and her immediate loved ones, has taken the time and effort to care for others. She is understandably a vivacious, energetic woman.

The Karmic Law which none of us can adequately explain, works despite human intellection. *How* it works is nothing short of miraculous.

Do you want a strong, healthy body? Give the lame and the crippled a helping hand.

Do you want a strong, healthy mind? Help the mentally ill, the retarded and the blind.

Do you want a strong, healthy soul? Succor the depressed, the hopeless and the despondent.

Read and utter the Health Creed daily; reactivate your sense of empathy, the caring for others and let the Healer of life and limb infuse your life with vivacity, vitality and strength.

HE AVOIDED HIS AUNT LIKE THE PLAGUE

James V., of Lincoln, Nebraska, requested that I publish his letter to me for the benefit of others. I do so with gratitude:

June 7, 1975

Dear Mr. Laurence,

I started using the Health Creed because my blood pressure was very high and I feared an imminent heart attack. Worrying about it only made my condition worse. I was worried because I knew that if I suffered a stroke my family would suffer monetarily and morally. Before I heard the lectures you gave here I was trying to avoid everything that I felt was hurting my chances of recovery.

That's where my aunt and the Health Creed come in. I was avoiding my aunt like the plague because she is terribly ill and just to be near her depressed and worried me and I had this strange feeling that if I stayed around her too long I'd get as sick as she is. What horrors come from man's breast!

You put me on the right track. I started saying the Health Creed with all my heart. Two days later I couldn't wait to get to my aunt's house! I read aloud to her for hours. I fix her tea. I sit with her and talk with her and visit two and three times a week. Now I find that I'm the *only* relative who cares for her. It seems like everyone has been avoiding her!

I just want you to know that this poor old woman will never be alone in the world again, not as long as I have two feet to carry me to her bedside.

I also want you to know that my last visit to the doctor's office revealed that my blood pressure is normal! The doctor jokingly asked me if I had been doing yoga exercises or something. I told him about the Health Creed. He was so interested that he's interested in passing it on to many of his patients. Please write to him and let him know that you are agreeable to this and that he needn't worry about copyright or anything like that. I know you aren't the kind of person who presses such matters.

Cordially yours,

James V.

I of course complied with James' wishes and permitted the good doctor to use the Health Creed in his practice. James' P.S., however, was the most important part of his letter. It said: "I haven't felt healthier in years!"

WHAT HEALTH REALLY IS AND HOW
TO GET IT AND KEEP IT

Health is the Condition of Wholeness, as the creed says. Wholeness, however, is a gift to humanity from on high, that is, wholeness comes from within. You cannot manufacture wholeness, health, vitality, energy, vim and vigor. The ancient mystics have often said: "The things which are seen are but a mirror of the things which are not seen." This is nowhere truer than in your daily life. Everything you see with your eyes is a reflection of something not seen, something within yourself—within your Self. What obtains in the Self reflects outside. This is why the mystics also say: "As above, so below." The Self is above, the world around you is below. If you want health, then help others, for others are reflections of your own unseen psychic contents. You see, it is the *reason* you help others that is important to you. Intent means more than charity. *Know* that when you help another human being you are helping yourself! Health and help should be wedded in your thoughts. Help others and you grow healthier!

8

How the Success Creed Brings You Riches and Abundance

The most vital—and the least acknowledged—power in the world is the power of belief. It is operating every minute of every hour of every day, whether we know it or not. When you mail a letter, you are believing you will get a reply. When you write a check you believe the bank will honor it. When you work a week you believe you will receive a paycheck. Indeed, when you arise in the morning you believe another day extends before you. We live in a world built on belief. And yet, it never ceases to amaze me how many people have lost the belief in success. Tight money, depressed conditions, poverty, high costs of living—all these things and more—undermine the power of belief in success, riches, and wealth. But the fact is: the greater the power of belief, the greater and richer your life.

WHY THEY LOST THEIR FAITH IN SUCCESS

I met with a small group of interested individuals in a private home in Atlanta, Georgia some months ago. The group was composed of four people, two couples: Don and Joyce S., and Eric and Jean F.

Don did not believe in success today, because "the economic situation militates against it."

Joyce's power of belief in success was undermined by her belief in "breaks and rules that favor the rich."

Eric didn't believe in success, because "I've been working steadily for ten years and what have I got to show for it? The more I earn, the higher prices go. How can I be a success?"

Jean had no faith in becoming successful, because "success comes only to a few in the world and I don't expect to be one of them!"

These otherwise sensible people lost their faith in their ability to achieve success because they were permitting exterior conditions and circumstances—not to mention prior programming—to short-circuit their own power of belief.

It was due to these despairing people, and others like them, that I developed the Success Creed to help them reactivate their power of belief and to get back in touch with the source of wealth and riches. These four people in particular came to know success after using the creed faithfully and by employing the "Six Steps to Success" which grew out of the Creed.

The Success Creed and the Six Steps are provided here for your use:

THE SUCCESS CREED THAT EXPLODES
IMPOVERISHMENT AND LACK

I *believe* in Success the Height of Achievement, Nemesis to lack and poverty:

And in Prosperity its obvious manifestation: which was once the hope of every man, produced through effort: undermined by lack of confidence, was doubted, delimited, and denied; it seemed beyond man's reach; in times of economic stress it beckoned anew: it called the unvanquished, and brightens the lives of any who attain Success the Height of Achievement: for them it shall bring progress and fortune.

I *believe* in Prosperity: the reality of Success; the joy of

accomplishment: the need for confidence: the re-establishment
of Prosperity: and in Success interminable.
Amen.

The "Six Steps to Success" grew out of the last part of the creed.
The six items listed became powerful meditation aids for reactivating
the power of belief. I first discussed them with the Atlanta group.

THE SIX STEPS TO SUCCESS AND
HOW THEY WORK

I advised Don and Joyce, and Eric and Jean to analyze the compo-
nents of the last paragraph of the creed and to concentrate on each.
We broke down the last part of the creed in this way:

I Believe in Prosperity
I said: "People all over the world are achieving success, why
shouldn't you? Yes, there is lack and poverty, starvation and
impoverishment. But so is there plenty and riches, accomplishment and abundance. You have to believe in one or the other.
Reaffirm your own power of belief. Repeat daily: I *believe* in
Prosperity."

I Believe in the Reality of Success
I said: "Never lose your belief in the reality of success. To the
degree that you lose that, to that degree you experience loss and
deprivation. Don't let appearances fool you: this world is prolific with wealth of all kinds. Draw some of it to yourself by
believing in success, no matter how things look. Success is real
and present. You can enjoy it, too, if you reactivate your power
of belief."

I Believe in the Joy of Accomplishment
I said: "Have you so soon forgotten that accomplishment is a
joy? When you glory in your achievements, no matter how small
they are or how insignificant they seem, you set up a karmic
reaction pattern of joyous giving. Stop belittling the things you
do, the work you undertake, the activities you perform. Take

joy and pleasure in all you undertake and you will be blessed with the divine feeling of joy."

I Believe in the Need for Confidence
I said: "Let's stop facing every day with drawn faces, sunken hearts, and defeatist attitudes. Never mind what things *look* like: let's you and I face each new day with enthusiasm, hope and trust. Let us be *confident* that whatever we undertake to do today will be positive, productive, and fruitful. Let's reaffirm our confidence in life itself, and then we will be permitting success and happiness to come to us."

I Believe in the Re-establishment of Prosperity
I said: "Are the prosperous sad and dejected? Are the prosperous crestfallen, enervated, worrying? Are the prosperous doubtful, defeated, alarmed? By no means! The prosperous are getting even *more* prosperous! You can do the same. Prosperity is available to all of us. Let us not forget that. Let us not doubt in the universality of Prosperity. Rather let us reaffirm our own power of belief and welcome Prosperity into our lives. *Believe* that Prosperity can be established and you will *receive* Prosperity."

I Believe in Success Interminable
I said: "The word 'interminable' means 'without end.' Success is ongoing, endless, unstoppable, immortal, if you will. You can enjoy success here and now, today, in your own life, if you will reactivate your power of belief in success. Why should you do without simply because certain ideas and attitudes prevalent today say success is out of your reach? It is *not* out of your reach. Success is as far away as your power of belief.

THEY AFFIRMED THEIR BELIEF
AND GREW RICHER

These affirmations helped the four people in Atlanta, as well as others around the states. Don and Joyce, Eric and Jean were test patterns in a way. Each affirmed his or her own power of belief and ceased to identify with lack and deprivation. One by one they began

to experience changes in their lives, sometimes in big ways, sometimes in small ways, but always in successful ways.

Don's income increased after three weeks. Joyce's knitting and
crocheting brought her extra money. Eric sold his coin collection and
discovered that among the many coins was one of supreme value.
Jean received an unexpected windfall.

Don now makes almost $12,500 annually. Joyce wrote and said:
"I can't tell you how good it feels to have my own money. It tickles
me pink every time I look into my purse. There's always at least a
twenty-dollar bill there, every day!"

Eric had decided that saving coins was now a very expensive
hobby and he sold it to gain extra income. It was a good collection,
saved over many years, and he expected at least $8,000 for it. To his
complete surprise, just one single coin in the collection sold for
$7,500!

Jean's story is remarkable. She had applied to a television network
as a potential contestant on a popular quiz program. She was accepted
and flew to New York and appeared on national television as a
contestant. She won a new refrigerator, skis, a motor boat, a fur coat,
a year's supply of soups, tickets to theaters, shoes, gloves, a neck-
lace, and many more gifts. The total worth, she wrote to say, was
over $10,000. She said: "I was so excited during the show that I
thought I'd burst a blood vessel. But I kept repeating over and over in
my head, 'I *believe* in Prosperity, I *believe* in Prosperity.' And I do!"

WHY THE SIX STEPS TO SUCCESS AND THE
POWER OF BELIEF ARE AN UNBEATABLE COMBINATION

David B. is a youth volunteer who does typing of correspondence
for me when I am in Washington, D.C. Dave is only eighteen years
of age, but he has been practicing the Success Creed since he was
seventeen, and receiving many signs of success. Every night before
retiring Dave reiterates the Success Creed in its entirety.

An interesting chain of events makes Dave's personal story inspiring. You see, it was part of his job to answer my correspondents when I was too busy to do it myself. Dave came to me when he had the free time to devote to my office work. He got the free time because he hurt his leg one day and was laid off his job. But he told me: "None of that bothered me. I just kept saying, 'I believe in Prosperity.' " I offered to pay Dave $20 a day for helping me. He refused the money. He said: "I appreciate the offer, but I'm working on *big* prosperity. I'd just like to help you while I'm waiting for it to happen to me."

The chain of events, beyond his knowledge or mine, was already in operation. David had been secretly corresponding with one of my Ohio clients, a nineteen-year-old girl named Joan D. Now, Joan was using the Love Creed, trying to bring true love into her life in Ohio. Here in Washington, Dave was using the Success Creed, trying to bring Prosperity into his life. The two apparently came together in another realm.

When David told me one day that he had fallen in love, I was happy for him. But when he told me it was Joan D., of Ohio, with whom he had fallen in love, I was astounded. They had never met! But Dave showed me a stack of letters and I had to admit at least speculatively that this young couple had found each other via air mail. But I also knew something that David did not, something which Joan did not tell him in her lovely letters. Joan D. is the daughter of a multimillionaire.

Now some people would like to believe that David married Joan for her money, but I know both of these young people personally. I have seen their power of belief at work in their lives, and I have seen how the Unconscious works in mysterious ways.

Joan D. was rewarded for her belief in Love. She married the young man she chose to marry. And David was rewarded for his belief in Prosperity, for that is exactly what he has today. One of his letters was fair to bursting with his irrepressible glee. His new father-in-law had given him a Rolls-Royce—not for a wedding gift—but simply because he liked David. Prosperity is in the palm of young David's hand now.

HOW THE POWER OF BELIEF WORKS FOR YOU TO BRING YOU SUCCESS

The power of belief I speak of in these pages is not based upon religious principles *per se*. It does not rely upon creeds, dogmas, rituals or traditions. When I speak of *your* power of belief, I refer to a mental attitude, a faith in Unconscious potentiality. Your power of belief penetrates the deepest layer of your psyche and the all-embracing Unconscious responds accordingly.

> . . . According to your faith be it unto you.
> —Matthew 9:29

The above Bible passage records a universal truth. Reactivate your power of belief, affirm your faith in Success, Prosperity, Plenty and Abundance, and your Unconscious can respond by giving you these very things.

You can rise above the pervasive miasma of gloom that suffocates so many people today. By using the Success Creed and the Six Steps to Success, by infusing them with your power of belief, you can accomplish, achieve and excel.

Ted L., of Grant's Pass, Oregon *believed* in Success and became a motion picture star.

Helen R., of Monterey, California *believed* in the joy of accomplishment and graduated from college with honors.

Gene A., of Pittsburgh, Pennsylvania *believed* in confidence and became a successful writer of positive-thinking literature.

Harold P., of Austin, Texas *believed* in the re-establishment of Prosperity and emerged from a state of bankruptcy into a rich real estate developer.

Beverly N., of Santa Fe, New Mexico *believed* in Success interminable and went from part-time waitress to part-time model to full-time model to stage actress to producer and director, and finally to owner of her own theaters.

You can add your name to the list of happy and prosperous people when you awaken dormant powers of belief, when you practice the Success Creed with feeling, hope and expectation.

Use the creed every day or night and continue to look forward, onward and upward. Success is real!

9

How the Energy Creed Empowers You to Overcome Affliction and Psychic Attack

Today, more often than not, psychic attack comes from within ourselves, not from outside. In past centuries it was known that psychic attack came predominantly from exterior sources: enemies, sorcerers, evil-doers, malevolent individuals and negative people. Modern psychology does not rationalize these sources away, but it reveals that psychic attack can very well come from within also.

When you are undermined psychologically your strength and vitality is depleted, leaving you susceptible to many kinds of illness: colds, headache, nervous conditions, etc. A moral defeat or a loss of prestige can erode one's personal sense of power and endurance.

A recent editorial in the Orlando, Florida *Sentinel Star* reported: "Richard Nixon's political fall has been a terrible ordeal for him . . . There is speculation that the former president was so devastated psychologically by Watergate that he no longer has the will to survive this illness.''

If you ever wondered what you have in common with presidents and kings it is your susceptibility to disease, enervation and psychological devastation. Great men and small alike are equally subject to defeat and equally capable of victory. The secret lies in knowing where the center of force and power lies. When we know that it lies within ourselves we can get in touch with it, tap it and enjoy it in this life. You overcome affliction and psychic attack to the degree that you channel life-giving, energy-producing forces from within.

HE SAID: "I'LL NEVER GET BACK ON MY FEET."

Doug M. is a young college student in Amherst, Massachusetts. Until quite recently he was vigorous, active and energetic. Then he learned that his girl friend back home in Wisconsin, who had presumably been waiting for him, had married another man. Doug was crushed psychologically by this turn of events. He grew listless, disinterested and lackadaisical. He lost weight, energy and get-up-and-go. He grew so weakened that he was no longer fit to play basketball or football.

It was his worried parents who called me to Massachusetts. When I saw Doug he was but a specter of what he looked like in earlier photographs. But it wasn't as though he hadn't tried to get a hold of himself.

He said: "I know I shouldn't let this thing get me down. I've tried dating other girls; tried to forget Ellen. But something is wrong. When Ellen left me, something else left me, too."

It became apparent that when Doug lost his love, he lost his own contact with his strength and will. I explained to Doug that he could not permit a single life-event to completely enervate him. I prodded him to re-establish his knowledge of the center of energy within.

I said: "While dating, working and sports participation may divert your mind from your problem, they will not put you back in touch with your own reservoir of vitality and dynamism. *You* have to do that."

To help Doug I gave him the Energy Creed and instructed him to say it with meaning and emotion every night before retiring. He followed my instructions to the letter and was better off for it. In a matter of days he was recovering facial color; in weeks he was animated again, eyes reflecting inner strength; and in just months he was jolly, alive, happy and enjoying life as a young man should be enjoying life.

THE CREED THAT INFUSES YOU WITH ENERGY

Here is the creed I gave to Doug. Say it with feeling, mentalize it, recite it orally, and you will find yourself receiving new surges of strength and vitality.

> I *Believe* in Energy the Cosmic Force, Potency behind the seen and the unseen:
> *And* in Power available to man: emanating from Above, reflecting Below: displaced by skepticism, was underestimated, disdained, and spurned: it waned; it imbues the elect: it charges the being, and fills the soul with Energy, the Cosmic Force: it desires to uplift the weak and the helpless.
> I *believe* in Power: dynamic energy; personal vigor and charisma: the conquest of impotence: the presence of superpersonal strength: and in Energy undying.
> *Amen.*

HOW A MODEL EARNS $100 AN HOUR!

Joy T., of Nashville, Tennessee has not been psychologically devastated by anything in her life, but she uses the Energy Creed faithfully. Joy is a voluptuous redhead, twenty-two years old. She is a model. Her stock in trade is beauty, vivacity and glamor. She possesses these things and has no intentions of losing them or taking them for granted. A sensible girl, Joy realizes fully that the modeling field is a highly competitive one. If she is going to continue to earn $100 each hour that she is under the lights, then she must preserve her important assets.

Joy said: "I say the Energy Creed every day, sometimes twenty or thirty times, I guess. I say it to myself when I'm working, believing that my inner strength and power will show up in the pictures. According to critics, it does! Maybe I'm vain, but I don't care. I like being beautiful and attractive and if the Energy Creed will help me to remain so I'm all for it."

The last time I saw Joy she had just finished an afternoon's shooting, a matter of three and a half hours' work. Joy was $350 richer than she was at lunch!

THE COSMIC FORCE OF ENERGY
AVAILABLE TO YOU

To many people, energy is something produced by machines and electricity. Energy, however, is infinitely more than that. Energy was present in the universe long before man ever evolved. What man does is *tap* the source of that energy and channel it for his own uses. All he *can* do is channel it; he cannot manufacture it. This is why even today, in this modern technological age, scientists still do not know what electricity is. They only know that it is a power and that it works. Energy in and of itself is an invisible agency. Nothing can contain it, confine it or imprison it. Energy is without and within, permeating everything, pervading the very atmosphere. Internal energy is called psychic energy.

No scientist has ever seen Energy, but we can use this potent agency in all areas of our lives. You need this inner storehouse of Cosmic Force if you are going to be successful at anything in this life. Goethe wrote:

Energy will do anything that can be done in this world; and no talents, no circumstances, no opportunities, will make a two-legged animal a man without it.

HOW YOU CAN DRAW UPON COSMIC FORCE

You can draw upon Cosmic Force, the Energy within you and accomplish anything in this world. I have been to many cities in this country and I have met many people, but I have never yet met a person who operates at his or her optimum without tapping the inner source of strength and vitality. These people are the ones others look upon in admiration, and exclaim, "I wish I had that much get-up-and-go!"

As you practice the Energy Creed, letting the Unconscious know you are attentive and receptive, you will discover that this miraculous Cosmic Force can empower you, propel you toward success, energize your mind and body, and keep you from illness and depression, lack and limitations. This inexorable Cosmic Force—Energy—can infuse you with self-direction (Self-direction) and guide you to new avenues of personal expression. You can possess vitality, charisma, character, creativity and vigorous spirit which combine to make you happy, successful and important to others.

HOW HER POWER OF BELIEF GAVE
HER THE ENERGY TO MAKE MONEY

I knew Alice N. only vaguely as a regular and familiar face at the lectures I held in Scottsdale, Arizona six different times over a period of a year. She seemed to be doing well. But I sensed there was something wrong somewhere. While she seemed to understand everything said, and while she averred that she was practicing the techniques, I could not help but notice that she often looked pale and drawn. During my last visit to Scottsdale I made it a point to talk with her. She was friendly and amiable, gracious and kind. She invited me to her home for dinner and there I met her husband, a young man of good character. But I met with something unexpected. Alice, it seemed, was an inveterate pill-taker. I was shocked to learn that she was dependent on two or three different kinds of "uppers," pills for inducing false energy.

Her husband said, "I'm sure glad Alice invited you here. Maybe you can talk some sense into her. She won't listen to me. She likes to pretend that the pills don't matter, but behind her facade of strength and vigor is a wasting young girl."

I asked Alice if she was really interested in tapping the inner source of Energy. She claimed that she was indeed. Taking her at her word, I got strong with her.

I said, "Then the first thing you do is throw those pills away."

I asked her to produce them, and she did—blue ones, green ones, yellow ones—and I scooped them up in one hand and chucked them into the garbage. Alice looked somewhat shocked and not a little dismayed. Her husband was telling me that Alice works at home while he is at the office. She weaves. "But," he told me, "she doesn't have the strength to produce the lovely things she likes. She's been too tired lately."

All that has changed now, after a few months of using the Energy Creed *faithfully*, without recourse to pills. Alice is vivacious, bubbly and energetic, and she produces marvelous woven pieces. She wrote to me recently, and here is what she said:

> I thought those pills were helping me. They were holding me back! I can't believe the difference between the energy I thought they were giving me and the Energy coming from within. I've been working so fast people are amazed at my productivity. I sold a piece just last week for $135. Two days ago another sold for $150. And yesterday a lady came by and commissioned me to weave her a wall-hanging, and she advanced me $400! I'm still practicing that fantastic Energy Creed and the Cosmic Force is still flowing!

HOW THE ENERGY CREED OPENS DOORS
TO FULFILLMENT AND SUCCESS

Alice's is not an isolated case. I know men and women all over the United States who have reaffirmed their power of belief and then practiced the Energy Creed to put themselves in touch with the inner supply of Cosmic Force.

Curtis F., of Little Rock, Arkansas, works in a steel mill. He was bored to death with his job and failing miserably at it. He was the lowest paid employee, earning $2.25 per hour in the least productive job in the business. He and I talked a great deal and we traced his boredom, not to a boring job, but to his own lack of interest and elan. He practiced the Energy Creed for weeks and continues to do so today. He is now the company's most valued employee, so valued that he is paid $6.50 per hour now.

He said: "I don't work like a horse like the other guys, but I produce more than any one of them—and I've got energy to spare!"

Another case is that of Tony P. Since he has been tapping his reservoir of strength and vitality he has won every amateur boxing match he's been in. He was previously known as the "Horizontal Kid."

Ethel C., of Salt Lake City, Utah, said to me: "I love ice-skating. I once had the vision of being a star, but the practice requires more energy than I have. I guess I'll settle for less than stardom."

I said: "With that attitude, stardom will forever be beyond your reach. If you are adept at ice-skating, if you really like it, then go after the brass ring. Don't undersell yourself like that. If it's energy you need, tap into your own source and supply."

I taught Ethel the Energy Creed. She reactivated her power of belief, affirming, "I *believe* in Power: dynamic energy; personal vigor and charisma: the conquest of impotence: the presence of superphysical strength: and in Energy undying. *Amen.*"

She resumed her ice-skating practice and, if local newspaper write-ups are any indication, she is a star in the making.

HOW TO PRACTICE THE ENERGY
CREED EVERY DAY

You can tap an impressive amount of Energy and benefit from it in your own life. Reaffirm your *belief* in extra-human Force and you will receive it. Don't undersell yourself. Get in touch with your inner dynamo now!

10

How the Sustenance Creed Multiplies Riches and Increases Wealth

More and more people today are saying to me: "We really want the good things of life, but they're too expensive. We have faith, we hope, we trust, and yet the riches and wealth fall to others." And they usually ask: "Why?" I then reply: "Why do you think?" The answers I receive are revealing. Some say, "Because the wealth of the nation can be spread only so thin." Others say: "I can't compete with the money-grubbers." Still others say: "I can only make so much on my job! How am I going to get rich by working like a horse for peanuts?"

All of these answers from sincere and trustful people indicate one primary thing: a lack of belief in eternal Sustenance. People become deluded by appearances. The news media cry: "Recession! Depression!" and people everywhere *believe it* so deeply that they undermine their own faith in the Source of all wealth. Certainly these are hard times. Yes, prices are higher than ever. Yes, paychecks look lean compared to costs. But the fact remains that the source of eternal

Sustenance knows no lack. What does the giver of all know of recessions and depressions? Does the religionist doubt God in times of stress? Hardly. Faith is the answer. Your power of belief in unending riches and a steady flow of wealth opens channels for the very manifestation of these things.

THE SOURCE OF RICHES AND PLENTY

We tend to let circumstances dictate to us. We see lack, hear of lack, and subsequently *believe* in lack. Then we experience lack. And even as we experience lack, the source of riches and plenty is still intact, still overflowing, seeking an outlet. You can be that outlet. As you go about your daily life, *believe* you are in the presence of the wealth-source. Rechannel your power of belief and believe that the Giver of All is right with you, knows your needs, wishes you well, and delights in supplying you with whatever you want. First and foremost, reactivate your power of belief.

THE CREED OF SUSTENANCE AND HOW TO USE IT

The Sustenance Creed may be viewed as an affirmation of an infinite storehouse of riches in your Unconscious, which responds to your material needs to the degree that you permit it to. You permit it to operate by believing in its power to provide, bless, give, flow, and imbue you with riches. The Unconscious knows no limitations. It knows nothing of setbacks, poverty, hard times, and crises. Get in touch with this mighty center of abundance by reciting the Sustenance Creed, which reactivates your power of belief in the source of goods and possessions. Affirm:

> I *believe* in Sustenance the Divine Support, Obstacle to poverty and destitution:
> *And* in Income its physical form: which is fundamental reinforcement, designated for man: suffered under economic stress,

was reduced, taxed, and rendered inadequate: it failed to meet basic human needs; to the persevering it is still available: it can be increased, for it is the product of Sustenance the Divine Support: it can lighten the burdens of the spiritless and the pauperized.

I *believe* in Income: increased wealth; more money and goods: the improvement of circumstances: the multiplication of riches: and in Sustenance eternal.

Amen.

YOUR POWER OF BELIEF AND YOUR WEALTH ARE INTIMATELY CONNECTED

As you reaffirm your belief in eternal Sustenance as the indefatiguable source of all wealth, you will find new power at work for you and all around you. Exactly *how* the Unconscious works in this way no one knows, but *expect* results. These may come through fellow human beings, or pay raises, or contest winnings, or even surprising windfalls. The more you *believe* in the Divine Source of Support and its ability to help you, the greater are your chances and opportunities for accruing wealth.

To help you re-establish your power of belief even in the face of lack and deprivation, affirm often:

I *believe* in Income: increased wealth; more money and goods: the improvement of circumstances: the multiplication of riches: and in Sustenance eternal. *Amen.*

DIVINE SUPPORT REVEALS ITSELF IN MYSTERIOUS WAYS

After you have reactivated your power of belief and affirmed the efficacy of Divine Support, you must be prepared for surprises. Your needs are not always met in ways you might expect, nor does Divine Support manifest as you might think. If you are not open, expecting, and waiting with anticipation, you may miss opportunities and blessings which the Unconscious has set up for you. Keep an open mind and an expectant heart. Be prepared for anything to happen in your life to sustain you, enrich you, and increase your wealth.

FIVE SIMPLE WORDS MADE HIM RICH

Matthew D. worked the night shift in a Des Moines, Iowa factory. He worked hard to support his wife and two children. When hard times came the D. family was living hand-to-mouth. Although he was under great economic pressure, Matthew never let his children know it. He kept the faith, and he faithfully practiced the Sustenance Creed daily. On Saturday mornings he could be found with his children on the living room floor, laughing and playing games. While he was shielding his loved ones from the cruelties of life, he himself was affirming the reality of Divine Support and waiting expectantly for aid. At this time, Matthew had exactly fifty-three dollars in the bank. His rent is $175 per month. Food alone costs him anywhere from thirty to fifty dollars a week.

One fine Saturday morning a co-worker dropped by to visit. This man saw Matthew playing a game with his children and mentioned that he'd never seen such a game before. Matthew modestly admitted that he had made it himself for the kids, something they enjoyed tremendously. The visitor was impressed, and he said five words which were to change Matthew's life forever. The visitor said: "Why don't you market it?"

Matthew said to me: "I'd heard that one before. I've made lots of games and toys for the kids. But this was different. When my friend said those five words I was already practicing the Sustenance Creed. I was ripe for word from the Unconscious. I was ready for mysterious aid. When he said those words, it sounded like they came from inside me instead of outside. I told him that I knew nothing of marketing things and he suggested I stop by the local college and ask around.

Well, I did, and I got some fabulous information, and I marketed the game."

Matthew's game is now in stores all over the country. It sells for $10. Matthew's share of the profits is 30 percent, which means that he makes $3 on every sale. Now, that may not sound like much, but pause and consider that Matthew's very first royalty statement reflected the sale of 50,000 games. At 30 percent, Matthew realized an income of $150,000! And the game is just starting to gain in popularity. When I heard from Matthew last, he was producing another game! He had *expected* to hear from the source of plenty and he did.

HE SAID HE HAD ABSOLUTE BELIEF
IN THE POWER OF DIVINE SUPPORT

Andy S. had a poor-paying job that only seemed worse when prices rose. Clothing, rent, utilities and even food were fast getting out of his reach. But Andy was already practicing the Sustenance Creed, activating his power of belief and trusting in the powerful Unconscious to work miracles.

One day Andy came to tell me that he and his wife had decided to move to St. Paul, Minnesota, where they thought prospects would be better. I said to Andy: "Watch for the Unconscious in this decision."

When I visited St. Paul to speak about the Power of Belief, I dropped by to see Andy at his home. He and his wife were still struggling to make ends meet, even though Andy did have a better job as an office clerk.

He said: "I applied for a managerial position, but I'm a clerk."

I said: "Watch for the Unconscious. In spite of your feeling that *you* decided to move here, the Unconscious is behind all that you do. Remain expectant."

I received a phone call from Andy not long after, in which he told me that a difficulty had arisen. Andy's wife was exhibiting some jealousy because Andy's boss's wife was taking interest in him. As shady as this situation could sound to others, I said: "Watch for the Unconscious."

I wanted Andy to realize beyond a doubt that the Divine Support can act in strange and mysterious ways. When I visited Andy's home again, I found his wife cool and reserved towards me. She all but accused me of encouraging Andy to flirt with danger to home and hearth. I could understand her uneasiness, but there was nothing I could say to defend myself. My defense was not the issue. The richness and happiness of this young couple was the issue. I repeated to Andy in private: "Watch for the Unconscious."

I left St. Paul in February. Late in March I received the following letter from Andy and his wife:

> Dear Mr. Laurence,
> I followed your advice to the letter. With prices soaring and work a bore, with Linda nagging at me and worrying needlessly, I stuck it out and kept "watching for the Unconscious" as you put it. You will be happy to learn that my boss's wife is a wonderful, helpful individual. It was through her appreciation of my abilities that I am now being advanced to the managerial position I wanted in the first place. She informed her husband of "a hard-working, dedicated employee in the outer offices." That's me! The boss acted on his wife's suggestions and made me the office manager of the Sales Department. I'm now located on the fifth floor with a plush office of my own, and my salary is now $750 a month! I can't thank you enough for your moral support during my hard times. But I'll let Linda write now, because she is eager to.

> Dear Mr. Laurence,
> Can you bear to hear from a silly female? I can't tell you how happy I am that you encouraged Andy to stick with his principles and beliefs. I've been a perfect *monster* to him lately, and all because of my overactive imagination. I thought that Mrs. L. was . . . well, I won't go into that now. You know how I felt and believed. How horrid I was. Andy was right to stick to his

guns, and now things are looking up, thanks to him and to you.
Mrs. L. really did have maternal interest in Andy, no more and
no less, and she has been wonderful to us.

Can you ever forgive me for treating you so shabbily? I'll
know you forgive me if you show up at the house-warming of
our new home.

Love,

Linda and Andy

I cannot help but mention that the house-warming was a glorious
affair, a well-attended, happy occasion. Moreover, its posh and
glamour more than showed the results of Andy's power of belief.
Everywhere I looked in the new home there was nothing but the
finest. And midst all the gleam and glitter stood two smiling, happy
faces.

THE MAGIC OF SYNCHRONICITY

Some people like to believe that by uttering certain magical words,
wonderful and marvelous things will happen in their lives. But it is
not words that hold magic for you. It is your connection with the
magical realm of the Unconscious. When you use any of the creeds in
this book, you are not uttering magical words; you are tuning in to a
universal system of correspondences—and *this* is magical. When you
affirm your power of belief and use the creeds, you make contact with
pre-existent psychic patterns which in turn reflect in your outer life.
I'll give you some examples to illustrate this difficult to explain
psychic system.

Susan T., of Boise, Idaho, mentalized the Sustenance Creed
during breakfast one morning. On her way to work, five blocks from
the house, she dropped her purse. When she stooped to retrieve it, she
found a fifty-dollar bill!

Chance? Coincidence? Happenstance? No. This is what C. G.

Jung calls "meaningful coincidence." And meaningful coincidence in other terms is synchronicity. It may be defined as those instants when two apparently unrelated phenomena come together to produce a meaningful experience. Susan dropped her purse. She found a fifty-dollar bill. Two separate and unrelated phenomena came together for her—to her own good! This is the Unconscious at work. Magical? Yes! The Unconscious is magical when you let it be. It was magical for Susan. Scores of people were on the same sidewalk with her. None of them saw the money on the ground. Susan herself might have walked right over it. But she was not tuned in to the exterior world of appearances; she was tuned in to the inner world of reality. Anyone familiar with the term "Freudian slip," knows what I mean when I say the Unconscious *wanted* Susan to drop her purse at *that* time, in *that* place, for *her* benefit. The dropping of the purse—one phenomenon—linked meaningfully with the finding of money—another phenomenon. This is the magic of synchronicity.

HOW A YOUNG MAN GOT THE JOB
THAT SUITED HIM BEST

Earl E., of Lancaster, Pennsylvania, was standing for more than an hour on the unemployment line, waiting to apply for a job—any job, just so long as he could get to work and earn some money. He is a constant reciter of the Sustenance Creed. While on this long waiting line, Earl *chanced* to meet an old friend, who *happened* to mention a job in town. For Earl this was meaningful coincidence, not just another element in a routine life. Earl was tuned in to the Unconscious, expecting to hear from It. And he did. He left the employment office even though he was finally close to be interviewed. He marched out of the building, caught a bus, went straight to the company his friend had idly mentioned, and he obtained a position with that firm which makes him very happy and provides the income he desired.

EXPECT MEANINGFUL COINCIDENCE
WHEN YOU ARE IN NEED

A happy and successful friend of mine in Miami, Florida tells me that he now rarely plans anything, but relies heavily on Unconscious guidance, prodding, and events. When trouble, worry, or financial difficulties come his way, he recites the Sustenance Creed with feeling and invariably "something" happens to help him. He *expects* meaningful coincidences to occur.

When a financial problem appears, do not permit it to overwhelm you. Instead, reactivate your power of belief in abundance, recite the Sustenance Creed, and expect instant and miraculous aid. Do not be surprised if the answer to your problem comes through the telephone, or a letter, or a meeting. Anything can happen, and often does!

11

How the Purity Creed Gives Beauty, Charm and Personality

In this modern day and age it is no longer necessarily so that love and marriage go together like a horse and carriage, but changing times never alter one basic fact: beauty and success are related. Charm, charisma, good looks, attractiveness—these are things indispensable to successful living and loving. Many people are concerned about their looks, their appeal, their personalities, and rightly so. This is not vanity; it is common sense. We have to live among people who are influenced by and susceptible to charm and attractiveness. We therefore wish to be charming and attractive. There is nothing wrong in this.

WHY BEAUTY AIDS CAME TO FAIL

Flip through the pages of any leading national magazine and you will see a plethora of advertisements offering the "secret" to beauty, charm, popularity, and a host of other things. They rarely work, even though millions of dollars are spent in manufacturing them, advertising them, and purchasing them. I am not here denouncing commercial products. What I am doing is saying that this spray or that lipstick, this company's product or that manufacturer's lotion is not the "secret" to sustained and real beauty, glamour, or success in life.

I have already mentioned such words as "charm," "charisma," and "beauty." These things—and this *is* the secret—come from within. Attractiveness, radiance, good looks, personability, magnetism—none of these things can be applied like lotions, creams, and colognes. The only real beauty comes from a source hidden beneath our material facades, a place so deeply hidden in some people that they will never reach it or tap its power.

Beauty, I tell all of my friends, is the outer manifestation of inner Purity. Now I am not talking about chastity or holier-than-thouness or sinlessness. Purity is not something you have; it is something that *happens* to you. It is inner clarity, emanating from the Unconscious. It is inner Radiance, which emerges from psychic depths when we tap it. If you are in touch with this inner reservoir of Purity, you are attractive, truly attractive.

THE PURITY CREED THAT LINKS YOU WITH THE SOURCE OF BEAUTY AND PERSONAL MAGNETISM

People who depend solely upon artificial aids for their appearance are out of touch with the inner source of true beauty and personal magnetism. This is not to say that commercial products should not be used. Of course they should. But they should be exactly what they are called—*aids*—not sources. In other words, lotions, perfumes, lipsticks, colognes, and sprays are properly used when they enhance and complement *already existing* beauty. Pre-existent beauty is Purity, a spiritual or psychic condition.

Many people I know personally have used the Purity Creed to get back in touch with the internal source of Charm and Personal Magnetism. They have reaffirmed their power of belief and gotten back to basics, away from modern but sometimes erroneous beauty claims. They have learned the most important secret: even the most gorgeous hose will not transform ugly legs into beauties; the most expensive deodorant will not turn a grouch into an attractive man; the finest clothes in the world will not make a king of a peasant. Something vital is missing, something inner, something magical in a sense, which can and does transform the plain into the beautiful.

HOW TO TAP YOUR INNER SOURCE OF RADIANCE

Here is the creed that guides you to the real source of beauty, charm, and personality:

> I *believe* in Purity the Inner Source of Radiance, Precursor of vitality and personality:
> *And* in Beauty its outer unfoldment: which comes from within, emanating from the Unconscious: refuted by the worldly, was misapplied, misunderstood, and altered; it was deemed physical only; the enlightened ones tap its source; it emerges and blossoms into personality, and beautifies those who turn to Purity the Inner Source of Radiance: then to endow the person with character and attractiveness.
> I *believe* in Beauty: inner radiance; the real source of charm: transcendent qualities: the hidden genesis of personality: and in Purity inexhaustible.
> *Amen.*

THE BOSS WHO WAS DISLIKED BY EVERYONE

Herb G., of Roanoke, Virginia, is an employer who consistently alienated his employees. This unhappy, bilious man succeeded in spreading his cancerous unhappiness to his employees. He was always angry, insolent, difficult to please. One secretary finally quit, actually overcome by the man's terrible disposition, which created endless tension and unpleasantness in the offices.

Not a single woman in the company applied for the vacant position as secretary to Herb G. He was a despised man.

One day an outsider arrived, a lovely young woman named Betty R. Unbeknownst to anyone in the firm, Betty was a practitioner of the Purity Creed, a woman who knew that her beauty, charm, and personality stems from within herself. She came to the company happy, jovial, vivacious, quite different from the average person in the firm. Betty did not permit outer circumstances or conditions to sway her. She came to work early every morning, bright and cheerful. Her beauty overflowed into her surroundings. She brought flowers for Herb's office. She kept it tidy. His desk was always in neat order. In spite of Herb's nasty disposition, Betty persisted in inquiring about his needs, about how he wanted things done, pleasing him in spite of himself. Whenever she entered the office the room seemed to light up. By letting the Unconscious source of true Beauty flow through her, Betty transformed this wretched man into a considerate, happy person.

Employees were genuinely shocked to see Herb smiling during the day, sometimes chuckling. There was bounce to his step. And he did not delude himself as to how this transformation came about. He rewarded Betty for her contributions: She received raises quickly, and they were generous raises. When she started working, she was earning $300 a month. In less than a year she was taking home $700 a month, plus bonuses, gifts, and additional benefits. Betty continued to practice the Purity Creed, affirming her belief in transcendent Beauty and receiving it in body, mind and spirit. This happy condition at the office continued until Betty's husband was transferred to California, and she left the job to join him there.

Herb was visibly shaken by the fact that he was losing Betty, but he gave her a substantial going-away present: a check for $500. In a burst of appreciation and generosity Herb took the office personnel to lunch.

Betty was replaced by another woman, a woman who knew nothing of power creeds. Slowly but surely, Herb regressed to his original state of unpleasantness. He has since regained his reputation as the boss who is disliked by everyone.

GET IN TOUCH WITH PERSONAL POWER

Do you want to affect people the way Betty R. does? Perhaps you are a woman who wants your share of loveliness. Maybe you are a man who would like to be charismatic, attractive and appealing to the opposite sex. Then affirm: "I *believe* in Beauty: inner radiance; the real source of charm: transcendent qualities: the hidden genesis of personality: and in Purity inexhaustible. *Amen.*"

By making a habit of this affirmation, you welcome higher-than-human aid. In time you will feel the results: a stronger body, brighter eyes, color and exuberance. You can see the difference for yourself in your own mirror. The inner becomes outer. Inner Radiance becomes radiant personality. Inner Purity becomes outer looks. Inner forces emerge and manifest in your life as charm, personality and charisma. People begin to like you, look forward to seeing you, desiring your presence.

HE SAID: "I'VE NEVER BEEN MARRIED
AND ALREADY I'M 30!"

Glenn L. had a personal problem which is common to many men today. He just wasn't "hitting it off" with women, in spite of his worthy efforts. Glenn spends most of his hard-earned money on clothing—sharp-looking suits, fancy shirts, expensive shoes—and it was only after many years and many dollars that Glenn realized that he was never going to "make it."

He said: "Somehow I just don't seem to attract girls. Oh, they compliment me on my finery, don't think they don't. Lots of women have an eye for good things. But when it comes to *me*, the wearer of these fine duds, well, that's another story. Here I am thirty years old and I've never been married yet! And I've seen lots of women I'd love to be married to."

Glenn got in touch with his inner source of good looks and personal magnetism. He still looks fine in his dashing wardrobe, but there is something added. Glenn smiles and his eyes light up. He speaks and his voice mesmerizes. He glances at women and they are attracted to him as though he had cast a love spell over them. I've seen Glenn's address book and I can vouch for his seemingly outlandish claims to popularity. And one young miss who accompanied him to one of my lectures, told me: "When I'm with Glenn I feel like I'm with a real man."

What that young lady meant is important today. Women are no longer interested in clothes horses or men who come across as masculist, patriarchal, and authoritative. Real women are looking for men with inner qualities, sparkling personality, *true* good looks, not false images.

The converse is also becoming true. Many real men want real women, lovely women whose beauty is more than skin deep. The age of facade and make believe is over now.

The way to appeal today is to contact inner sources of natural and healthy looks and personality. The Purity Creed can be highly instrumental in putting you in touch with this Unconscious supply of charisma, charm, and attractiveness.

Glenn said: "I'm still not married, but I'm closer to it then ever before. The problem has changed, that's all. Before I wasn't married because I couldn't find a girl. Now I'm not married because I can't make up my mind which girl pleases me the most!"

TUNE IN, TURN ON, AND ENJOY LIFE

To borrow an ill-used phrase, you can tune in, turn on, and enjoy life when you realize that the qualities most sought for today come from within you. Your power of belief, that latent, dormant power, can be used to bring you not only a glamorous outer life, but astounding and captivating inner qualities.

Human improvement is from within outward.

—Froude

You must look into people as well as at them.

—Chesterfield

The qualities we have do not make us so ridiculous as those which we affect to have.

—La Rochefoucauld

There are many persons of whom it may be said that they have no other possession in the world but their character, and yet they stand as firmly upon it as any crowned king.

—Samuel Smiles

It is in men as in soils where sometimes there is a vein of gold which the owner knows not of.

—Swift

Many individuals have, like uncut diamonds, shining qualities beneath a rough exterior.

—Juvenal

Read the above statements carefully. Ingest them. They have been written by great men who knew the secret of inner strength, quality, and personality, and they have been preserved by men who recognize the truth of their meaning. Activate your power of belief, use the Purity Creed often, and you will tap the source of such qualities as these great men extol. Let true attractiveness, personality, and charisma come to life for you, imbue you, and make you pleasant to others. In turn, others will be pleasant to you. They won't be able to help themselves!

12

How the Cosmic Power
Creed Makes You Forceful
and Influential

In the preceding chapters we have discussed such subjects as Joy, Happiness, Truth, Wisdom, Good Luck, Love, Self-Confidence, Health, Success, Energy, Money, and Beauty. I have never yet seen a man who is happy, honest, wise, fortunate, self-confident, healthy, successful, energetic, and charismatic who wasn't also forceful and influential.

You should by rights be a force in your environment and influential with people around you. In order to be these things you must reach, tap, and channel the source of individual effectiveness.

In this age of mass-mindedness, too many people have stopped being individual, original, different. They have been swallowed up by the monster called collectivism. They have become numbers, statistics, mere working parts of a great machine. You do not have to suffer this fate.

WHY YOU SHOULD DEVELOP AND EXHIBIT
PERSONAL INFLUENCE

Today, more than ever before, competent leaders are needed. Not only as presidents and monarchs, but in every level of life. Look around you, read the newspapers, scan magazine articles. What do you see? I see more and more complaints about undependable men and women in business. Forthright individuals are called for. Energetic foremen are needed. Strong managers are unavailable. Reliable husbands, dependable laborers, productive workers, charismatic waitresses, confident employees—there is great demand for such as these now.

Opportunity is knocking right at this minute. You can now fill any one of thousands of lucrative and glamorous positions if you are the one needed, the one with personal influence, personality, energy, originality. Businesses are suffering all over the country from the dire lack of personable people. More and more people are suffering from lack of inner force. They appear in public like just so many empty faces, devoid of force and energy.

The cause of this widespread lack is that people have lost contact with the genesis of personal influence: Cosmic Force and Power. Their power of belief in inner sources of strength is deficient.

HOW COLLECTIVISM DESTROYS
INDIVIDUAL POWER

Too many people today look to technology and groupism as gods, answers to their personal needs. They want society to support them. They expect great things of the government. The "Company" has become God. In the process, their individual power is sapped, as though by some insidious parasite. They lose effectiveness, original thinking and the ability to act for themselves.

HIS IMPOTENCE WAS RUINING HIS LIFE

I met with Charles E. after a lecture in North Adams, Massachusetts. He was a distraught man, torn to pieces by feelings of inadequacy.

He said: "I feel like I'm drying up and dying. I used to be full of brilliant ideas. Now, I don't know what to think. I have a decent job, but it's so routine that I'm getting to feel like a vegetable. I work in a place with about twenty or twenty-five other people. We hardly know one another. We just work, poring over our duties like so many robots. I don't have any 'oomph.' And it's showing up in my married life. What is it that makes a man impotent?"

WHY A TWENTY-YEAR-OLD HOUSEWIFE
WAS CONTEMPLATING SUICIDE

A complaint similar to Charles's came to me from Edna I., of Peekskill, New York. She lamented that "life doesn't hold promise any more. I get up in the morning, fix my husband's breakfast, watch him drag himself to work, do the housecleaning, stare at TV, eat insipid food, and I wonder why? When I was eighteen, just two years ago, I felt ready to conquer the world. Look at me now, a mousy housewife with no more get-up-and-go than our lazy dog who lies around all day. What's worse is that recently I've been thinking strange things. I find myself wanting to end it all, because life doesn't seem worth living."

THE MAN WHO HAS EVERYTHING AND HATES IT

A letter from San Diego, California informs me that a man named Wayne Z. has everything he'd always wanted. He has a good job, a fairly good income, an apartment of his own where he lives alone by preference, a new television he just purchased, plenty of food to eat, dates, nightlife, excitement. But Wayne says he hates it all! Why? Because he doesn't *feel* alive. "Any zombie," he says, "can do what I'm doing. Something's gone out of my life."

THE DEVASTATED LIFE OF JOANNE P.

Joanne P. is thirty-two, a wife and mother of three, living in Butte, Montana. She wrote: "I used to be a very religious person. I had great belief in religion and in my preachers. Lately, though, my faith has been destroyed. When I read of how the Adam and Eve story is really a myth; when I hear that the Bible has been carefully chosen by men; when I see the bare lies and deceits I tell you I'm devastated! What is there to believe in these days? They say God is dead. Preachers and ministers all over the country are lying, marching in awful demonstrations, siding with corrupt politicians—what does it all mean? What is my life without my belief?"

THE POWER THAT NEVER DIES
WHICH YOU CAN TAP

These are but a few examples of the hopelessness and impotence pervading our society today. Now more than ever before we need good, strong individuals who can take the reins in homes, businesses, sports, politics, religion, and even in everyday person-to-person interrelationships. In order to reign, you must have power. In order to gain respect, you must have personal influence. In order to be important, whether to employer or employee, wife or next door neighbor, you must have force. The individuality and originality you want cannot be learned, purchased, or pretended. It comes from within, from the deep recesses of the Unconscious. In its original state, personal influence is known as Cosmic Power. They are one and the same thing, the one an obvious effect, the other an invisible cause. Cosmic Power filters down through the psyche to appear in you as personal charisma, force and influence. The way to receive this potent force is to tap your inner storehouse, the fount of Cosmic Power, and this can be done through the use of the Cosmic Power Creed.

THE COSMIC POWER CREED THAT RESTORES YOUR FAITH IN TRANSPERSONAL POWER AND IN YOURSELF

I *believe* in Cosmic Power the Ultimate Force, Devastator of impotence and weakness:
And in Personal Influence its immediate unfoldment: which is intended for all, born of Love: eclipsed by collectivity, was suppressed, repressed, and belittled: it was relinquished; in the era of groupism, individuals sought it afresh: it imbues seekers with strength, and it derives from the Cosmic Power the Ultimate Force: from thence it shall come to empower the oppressed and the downtrodden.
I *believe* in Personal Influence: individual effectiveness; the importance of originality: the depersonalization of collectivism: the reality of inner forces: and in Cosmic Power imperishable.
Amen.

HOW A YOUNG MAN OVERCAME APATHY AND ACHIEVED FAME AND FORTUNE

Jeff T. was a factory worker in Independence, Rhode Island when I first met him. Like many people I knew, he complained of a lack of effectiveness in the world. His job, he told me, was dull, exacting, and ill-paying. To add to his feelings of inadequacy he had certain people working against him. On previous jobs, like this one, he had been held back, denied promotions, refused raises. He was justifiably feeling persecuted and attacked. He told me of bosses who deliberately undermined his chances for advance. On his present job, he told me, fellow workers were generally negative, certainly not wishing him well. As a result of all his experiences, Jeff was downcast, lifeless and apathetic. He was, in short, giving up.

I counseled Jeff at great length. I explained to him that no matter how many people came against him, he had at his disposal a storehouse of energy, force and personal magnetism.

Jeff started using the Cosmic Power Creed nightly before going to sleep, saying it over and over in the quiet of his room. Once he had memorized it, he began reciting it mentally at work. In just days he began to feel an inner stirring, a movement of his spirit, an eruption he had experienced when younger, when he felt capable of facing the big world. Like a reborn man Jeff determined to do something with himself. If people were trying to attack him, he would remove himself from their attacks.

Jeff quit his job and moved to New York. He started his own mail order business. It was hard work and long hours, and he was making less money than ever. But he was no longer apathetic. He was feeling original and forceful. He had some ideas about this business and he started visiting local businessmen, rich and powerful men who could help him. Many were impressed with Jeff's self-confidence, his verve and his get-up-and-go. Two such rich men financed Jeff's business, giving him over $20,000 to get going.

Overnight, Jeff's mail order business began to flourish and show promising returns. He not only sold gewgaws and trinkets, but now expanded to supply customers all over the United States with the products manufactured by the men he had visited. In just weeks he went from a small store to three giant warehouses filled with thousands of dollars worth of material. Orders came in from everywhere and Jeff is raking in money, money, money. He now "thumbs his nose" (as he puts it) at those who had dared hold him back.

Jeff overcame his apathy and gained self-control, force and influence. He recites the creed daily now and continues to prosper.

In a matter of months Jeff has become the man Vergil wrote about in the *Aeneid:*

They attack this one man with their hate and their shower of
weapons. But he is like some rock which stretches into the vast
sea and which, exposed to the fury of the winds and beaten
against by the waves, endures all the violence and threats of
heaven and sea, himself standing unmoved.

You, too, can become Vergil's man. Get in touch with your source
of strength, overcome obstacles and excel.

13

How to Survive and Block Psychic Attack with the Guardianship Creed

We all know that we cannot like everyone. We also know that not everyone likes us. If we are mature we can accept these facts of life and go our own way. The dislike others may have towards us does not interfere with our own progress. Others have the right to dislike us. But they do not have the right to attack us, belittle us, or obstruct our progress. The most insidious kind of attack we can suffer is psychic attack. This kind comes from the invisible realm. We can feel it when we are objects of scorn, envy, greed, hatred and jealousy. Greedy people, jealous people, envious people and hateful people—all emit dangerous psychic waves which permeate the atmosphere and tend to affect our thinking, feeling and functioning. Who doesn't like the cheerful, positive-thinking individual?

Sometimes we do not know that we are under psychic attack. And yet, we may be getting bombarded by the most virulent emotions and feelings from those around us. We sit in movie theaters; we work in factories and offices; we mingle with strangers each and every day, on buses, in taxis, on the street and in stores. At any time negative energy can overtake us, leaving us depressed, angry, hostile and hopeless, without our knowing why we feel this way!

HOW AN AMBULANCE DRIVER DISPELS PSYCHIC BOMBARDMENT

Larry V. is a driver of an ambulance in Brooklyn, New York. He is surrounded by sorrow, misery and even death almost on a daily basis. Although it is certainly not the fault of his passengers, ailing and crippled victims—overcome by grief and pain—they emanate many negative feelings. Larry has felt these emotions as surely as he feels the steering wheel in his hands.

He said: "I've seen the worst things a man can see. In one day alone I saw the mangled body of a six-year-old girl who had fallen ten stories; a man bleeding to death from his suicide attempt; a fireman who had gotten his head crushed during a blaze; a policeman wounded in the stomach during a gunfight; a housewife burned in a house fire. But worse than this, I've seen the people around the victims—crying, fretting, looking fearful and doubtful—people who are potent broadcasters of negative emotions. Let me tell you, I *need* the Guardianship Creed. It protects me every day and night from negativity which these poor people don't know they are sending off."

WHAT IS THE GUARDIANSHIP CREED?

The Guardianship Creed is a particularly strong agent for fighting psychic attack of all kinds, whether this bombardment is accidental or deliberate. It is designed to put you in touch with Transpersonal Guardianship and protection. Guardianship, in its truest sense, is Cosmic Defense provided by Infinite Intelligence.

If you feel attacked by negative traits and characteristics; if you sense that you need a strong barrier against psychic bombardment; if

other psyches are invading your realm or disturbing your peace
—then the Guardianship Creed can be most vital to you.

Here is the Guardianship Creed that Larry uses:

YOUR PROTECTIVE INVISIBLE SHIELD

I *believe* in Guardianship the function of Infinite Intelligence,
Cosmic Defense against psychic attack:

And in Protection its invisible act: which is performed for the
faithful, born of concern: discarded by ego, was deemed naive,
impractical, and spurious: it fell into disuse; it became available
to new pilgrims: it secured the tormented, and all who need the
Guardianship function of Infinite Intelligence: from there it
shall preserve the attacked and the invaded.

I *believe* in Protection: the invisible barrier; the efficacy of
Infinite Intelligence: the perils of psychic attack: the power of
divine concern: and in Protection unending.

Amen.

THE DIFFERENCE BETWEEN THE VANQUISHED
AND THE VICTORIOUS

The vanquished people of this world no longer believe in Divine
Intervention into the affairs of men. Without this basic belief they are
cut off from Guardianship and Protection. They lay themselves open
to all the ills and errors of mankind. The victorious, on the other
hand, avail themselves of the divine gift of Cosmic Defense. They
know that it is the prideful ego which scoffs at the "superstition" of
Divine Guidance. They know that it is the ego which foolishly
plunges into dangerous situations and permits itself to be bombarded
indiscriminately by all sorts of negativity, for the ego likes to think
that it and it alone is in control of every situation. This attitude can
lead to disaster, obstacles, impediments and failure.

Those who know about Transcendent Forces also know that true
Protection comes from something higher than ego, from somewhere

in the unknown regions of the psyche. The re-establishment of your power of belief in Cosmic Defense will provide you with a protective barrier against psychic attack, no matter how strong that attack may be. Affirm: "I *believe* in Protection: the invisible barrier; the efficacy of Infinite Intelligence: the perils of psychic attack: the power of divine concern: and in Protection unending. *Amen.*" You will not be vanquished. You will be victorious.

HE SAW A COILING SNAKE COMING
TO GET HIM

It was only after Andrew T. had begun using the Guardianship Creed and feeling its beneficent activity in his life that he was able to tell me of his past experiences with evil and negativity. He told me of something that he describes as "a pattern of negativity."

He said: "For as long as I can remember I've had nothing but setbacks and obstacles in my path. I wanted to go to college but I couldn't. I had to work to help support my sick mother, because my father had died. By the time my mother was well again, it was too late to go to college. People told me to forget college, to stay home and take care of my mother. When I wanted to quit my job and look for a better one, well-meaning but regressive relatives told me to stick it out where I was. Things like this have happened to me for years. A few months ago, when I started using the Guardianship Creed, I began to see a pattern of negativity at work in my life. All of a sudden I realized that certain events throughout my life were taking on a set pattern. Relatives, loved ones, friends, acquaintances, even life itself, seemed to be working against me. Oh, they all said good-sounding things, but they were blocking me from advancing my own life. When I started reciting the creed every night, I had the unbearable feeling that a huge coiling snake was trying to devour me. That snake represents the series of events which have prevented me from progressing. I saw it in my vision as clearly as I see you now. It was hideous, a scaly monster with jaws wide and teeth dripping with saliva. It was going to get me if I didn't do something. I felt helpless before it. I needed a sword, like the heroes in mythology who confronted dragons. The Guardianship Creed has been my sword for weeks now and it cuts through obstacles like a fish fin cuts through water. Psychic attack has to be warded off, and the Guardianship Creed does that for me.''

HOW THE GUARDIANSHIP CREED CUTS THROUGH OBSTACLES

The Guardianship Creed can become your sword, too, when you reaffirm your power of belief in Transcendent Aid. This do-it-yourself age has led many people astray. There is a prevalent and fast spreading attitude abroad that man can do anything by sheer willpower alone, through ego-control. What a fallacy! I've seen too many suffering souls to believe in that, and I've seen too many vanquished people emerge as victors when they restored their faith in Greater-than-I forces.

You have to believe in Infinite Intelligence whose function is Guardianship and then you will know peace and prosperity. Then you will see the psychic atmosphere clear and the bright sun of clarity arise in your heart. The clouds of gloom and storms of negativity must be cleared. The Guardianship Creed acts as an effective agent against such delimiting and debilitating obstacles in your life.

HOW A LOS ANGELES MAN WALKS IN PEACE CONTINUALLY

Albert L., of Los Angeles, California, is a steady practitioner of the Guardianship Creed, and he agreed to come before a small group of us and tell of his experiences. He had mentioned that by using the Guardianship Creed he had come to know remarkable inner peace and safety, even in the face of various onslaughts.

He said: "I can best explain what I mean by talking about the movie *The Exorcist*. Everyone knows that this is a controversial movie, for more reasons than one. I wanted to go to see it. My aunt advised me against it, saying that it is horrible. She never saw it. I read in a newspaper that the movie evokes negative thoughts and feelings in people. A popular preacher who has a newspaper column said that it is sinful. Well, I was bombarded by all of this criticism and viewpoints until I was saturated by other peoples' ideas. I kept putting off seeing the movie myself. I was letting other people do my thinking and that aggravated me. I can think for myself. But I knew that if I was going to form a personal opinion of the movie, I would have to see it. At the same time I did not wish to be polluted by anything in the film. That's where the Guardianship Creed came to my aid. I recited it orally while driving to the theater and repeated it often mentally when inside the theater. I affirmed:

> I don't care what other people say, I am not going to be attacked psychically by this film. I *believe* in Protection: the invisible barrier; the efficacy of Infinite Intelligence.

"I felt that an impenetrable shield was around me as I watched this horrifying movie. People all around me were gasping and screaming, but I sat in peace and safety and digested the whole film without any adverse feelings.

"I learned a valuable lesson from this experience. I don't have to let other people tell me what to do or think or say. Protected by Infinite Intelligence I can do all things. This is just one example of how I use the Guardianship Creed. I use it in all areas of my life now and I walk in peace while others crumble and tremble around me. When I can and when I find a kindred spirit, I share the creed."

HE SAID: "SHIELA IS A PARASITE WHO SUCKS MY STRENGTH."

Alfred M. is an example of a man who had no conception of all of the dangers and perils of psychic attack. Alfred was totally attracted to another woman—Shiela—and he left his wife and children to live with this raven-haired beauty. In the end, Shiela led him to his own downfall. This is not to say that true love does not lead a man from one woman to another, nor am I delivering a moral judgment. Alfred was not directed by Love, but by lust, and that's another story entirely. Driven by his passion, he foolishly placed himself at the disposal of a beautiful but dangerous female. Shiela used him up. He lost weight. He grew nervous and irritable. He began to manifest jealousy at every turn and feared some other man might take Shiela away from him. And all the while Shiela was heartless, carefree and unconcerned about Alfred's well being. Here Alfred had thought he had the world by the tail. He believed that he was experiencing the fulfillment of his wild sexual fantasies. He thought he was living with the epitome of feminine pulchritude, a veritable centerfold girl! Actually, the spider-and-the-fly tale is more appropriate to describe Alfred's dilemma. He had all the sex he ever dreamed of, yes, but the total dedication to this hunger, to the exclusion of all other human needs, drove him almost insane. When he was a moral, mental and physical wreck, Shiela disappeared as mysteriously as she had appeared. Alfred returned to his wife a beaten man and it was only her true love that saved him from total annihilation. She nursed him back to health, cared for him, supported him, eased his conscience, and remained faithful to him. For it was she who was practicing the Guardianship Creed. Her own power of belief not only returned her husband to her, but afforded her psychic protection against the insidious thoughts and feelings of the woman who had destroyed Alfred.

HOW TO SURVIVE AND BLOCK PSYCHIC ATTACK

HOW TO ESCAPE THE CLUTCHES OF
PARASITIC PEOPLE

Shiela is a type of parasite. In this case we are talking about a woman who can easily sap a man of his energy, vitality and potency. But there are other kinds of parasites—rumormongers, liars, cheats, the jealous and the envious.

When Cosmic Defense is protecting you, you listen to people, talk with them, interact with them, but they are unable to undermine you, sap your strength or destroy your dreams. When you have divine protection you are safe from others who would consciously or unconsciously feed on your energy. When the Invisible Barrier is surrounding you, you can speak to such people but they cannot harm you. You talk with them, but you do not share your dreams. You meet them at work, in school and on the street, but you do not share your ideas with them. They are "unknowers." Your dreams, wishes, and ideas contain—indeed are composed of—your energy, and when others attack your dreams, wishes, or ideas, it is the same as attacking you with gun or knife or sword. It is worse, in fact, for psychic attack is so complete and so sly. It can appear in the form of a pretty face and a sexy body, as in the case of Shiela, or it can sound like good advice or seem harmless to you at first. The invisible Barrier protects you from all of these things.

HOW THE POWER OF BELIEF SLAYS DRAGONS

If you sense that some indescribable force is at play around you, recite the Guardianship Creed mentally or orally with feeling and you will instantly feel the difference in the atmosphere. You don't attack an enemy; your power of belief destroys that which would harm you. Affirm: "I *believe* . . ." and let higher-than-human forces go to work in your life to protect you, harbor you and embrace you.

14

How the Magnetism Creed Helps You to Overcome Lack and Deprivation

It is singularly remarkable how many people today have lost faith in Transcendent aid and support. Everywhere I go, from east coast to west coast, Canada to Mexico, I see sad eyes and wasted spirits. I see people suffering want and despairing of dreams. Destitution and poverty reign supreme, it seems. Whole groups of people and classes of people starve, and do without the necessities of life. Success and abundance are foreign words to them. Very infrequently do I meet a man or a woman who as an individual broke away from set patterns of destitution. Invariably, these shining lights in the midst of darkness *believe* in forces transcendent to those of which humans are capable. They have either retained or developed their power of belief.

HOW PATRICK F. OVERCAME HIS POVERTY-STRICKEN CONDITION

Patrick F. is a bus driver in Canton, Ohio. He came to me looking sorely distressed. He had lost faith in the transpersonal fund of abundance and plenty. He was mesmerized by reports of inflation, economic stress, and soaring prices.

I explained to Patrick that, despite all appearances to the contrary, there definitely is unlimited supply of riches, goods, and possessions. I implored him to reaffirm his power of belief, and reminded him of the dynamic force which can make things come to him and which can attract things to him. I told him he could become a veritable magnet himself and draw to himself all the wonderful things he wants out of life. And I impressed upon him that the source of this magical and miraculous magnetism is above and beyond human cognition.

I said: "If I told you that there is a warehouse just around the corner filled with all the things you want, would you believe me? And if I told you these things are there for the taking, would you believe me?"

Patrick laughed. No, he told me, he couldn't believe that. He looked genuinely shocked when I said: "Well, it's absolutely true."

I explained to Patrick that the warehouse was not around a physical corner, but was indeed just around a spiritual one.

I said: "Reactivate your power of belief. Trust in the Giver of All. Know that there is a vast storehouse of riches and abundance waiting for you, if you can but believe. Don't let modern pessimism eat away at your power of belief. It is the most valuable possession of all. With your power you can do all things, just like the Bible says. Get back in touch with the root source of all richness, wealth, and prosperity. You can have anything you want if you can believe it is yours."

To demonstrate the validity of my belief, I asked Patrick to name one thing he wanted badly. He said: "Well, off the top of my head, I guess I'd say a new car."

"Fine," I said. "Here's what I want you to do. Keep that new car in mind day and night. And as you do so, recite the creed I am about to give you. Utter it daily. Recite it before going to sleep. Think it through when you are working. Get your power of belief on the move."

THE CREED THAT DRAWS THE GOOD
THINGS OF LIFE TO YOU

Here is the Magnetism Creed:

I *believe* in Magnetism the Cohesive Force, Conductor of affluence and abundance:

And in Attraction its principal aspect: which is part of Cosmic Order, born of fundamental Law: obfuscated by mundane interests, was repudiated, rejected and eliminated: it became inoperative; despite man's folly it abides in Cosmos: it remains transcendent, and at one with Magnetism the Cohesive Force: from thence it shall respond to the needs of the impoverished and the destitute.

I *believe* in Attraction: Cosmic drawing power; the Law of Affinity: the conquest of lack and deprivation: psychic gravity: and in Magnetism unalterable.

Amen.

HE WANTED A NEW CAR AND DREW
IT TO HIMSELF

Patrick practiced the Magnetism Creed exactly three days when something fantastic happened to him. By utilizing this power creed he was sending out vibrations into the Cosmic Field, which responds like with like. This is the Law of Affinity.

After three days of reciting the creed, Patrick was called in to the main office. He was informed by his superior that the district manager had taken ill suddenly and someone was needed to undertake his responsibilities. Patrick had been chosen for this honor.

What astounded Patrick was that his duties consisted of traveling from bus depot to bus depot all over the city. He was to do this in a company automobile, provided for his use. The automobile was a brand new car. Not only this, but it was the color Patrick had been visualizing!

He said: "It's uncanny. After only three days I got the car I wanted. It *is* mine, for all practical purposes. I get to take it home. I'm permitted to use it privately. The gasoline is paid for by the company. I tell you, it's uncanny! Here I've got the new car I've been dreaming of and I don't even have to pay for it!"

BECOME A MAGNET AND ENJOY LIFE MORE ABUNDANTLY

It is imperative that you understand this basic principle: the Self (or God or Universal Mind, etc.) wants you to have what you need. Abundance, prosperity, goods, possessions, and all the good things of life come from within yourself. When you re-contact your own inner source of wealth, you become a magnet to attract to you all that you desire and need. The power of belief is essential to the operation of this psychic manifestation. Believe in wealth, abundance, plenty, and these things will be drawn into your realm of existence, sometimes in strange and mysterious ways, sometimes in quite unexpected ways. Once you have reactivated your power of belief, expect miracles.

HOW TO TURN A DULL LIFE INTO AN ADVENTURE

Re-establishing your power of belief revitalizes you and puts you back in touch with the primal source of all that exists. The Magnetism Creed puts you back in touch with that great center, the Unconscious, and this can make your life a wonderful adventure.

In *Man and His Symbols*, Dr. M. L. von Franz writes:

> Nowadays more and more people, especially those who live in large cities, suffer from a terrible emptiness and boredom, as if they are waiting for something that never arrives. Movies and television, spectator sports and political excitement may divert

them for a while, but again and again, exhausted and disen-chanted, they have to return to the wasteland of their own lives.

The only adventure that is still worthwhile for modern man lies in the inner realm of the unconscious psyche.

I have seen many such exhausted and disenchanted people in my travels across this country. Changing religious systems and moral values have undermined their faith in the transcendent, the superper-sonal, the divine. The psychology of Dr. Carl Jung has restored that faith in many lost souls. Turning to the Self, the source of all that is, they have found renewed hope in life.

When you reactivate your power of belief, turn to inner forces, unconscious forces, and embrace the Magnetism Creed, you can become a magnet which draws joy and happiness to you from every quarter.

WHY A HOPELESS CRIPPLE LAUGHS FOR JOY

Henry C., of Wallingford, Connecticut, is a Vietnam veteran. He is also a paraplegic, a man who is paralyzed from the waist down. When I first met Henry he was a mean-tempered, despondent and negative individual. He came to my attention through Barbara L., the young woman who loves him. Barbara came to me when Henry refused to see her any more. In great fits of self-pity, Henry banished her from his home and his heart, claiming that he was no good for her in his condition. Since he could not have sex, Henry felt that he would deprive Barbara of a full and satisfying life.

In tears, Barbara said to me: "Henry *makes* my life full and satisfying, just the way he is. Why can't he see that I love him and want to be with him?"

Henry was blind to more than Barbara's unselfish love. He was blind to higher forces. He was blind to the fact that Vietnam has produced many crippled men and that he is but one of many.

I worked with Henry for weeks. I taught him the Magnetism Creed and saw to it that he practiced it regularly. Barbara saw to that, even though her visits were not welcomed. I told Henry about the Unconscious, about the power of belief and about his own capacity for overcoming even his terrible ordeal. The alternative, I pointed out to him, was complete decay. Self-pity only breeds destruction. Henry had to get a hold on himself, take stock of his assets, not his debits, and go forward in this life.

Henry's re-establishment of the power of belief worked wonders immediately. He started to open up to the undying love of Barbara. She was soon welcome again in his home and thereafter in his heart. He didn't really want her to leave him alone. He needs her.

Once Henry permitted the Unconscious to activate in his life, once he gave up preconceived notions about what he could and could not do, wonderful things began to happen.

Henry and Barbara are now married, a powerful couple who bring aid and cheer to thousands of war veterans who are less fortunate. They visit hospitals in every state, encouraging defeated young men to bolster themselves, to look ahead and not back. Many people, afflicted and healthy, constantly remark about Henry's ultra-positive outlook on life, and they marvel that a hopeless cripple can laugh so much.

Henry is a happy man today. He thinks of himself, not as a cripple, but as a powerful agent of transcendent forces. He is an effective channel for Unconscious processes.

HOW THE POWER OF BELIEF MADE MAGNETS OF THEM

My files are thick with cases of people from all walks of life who have been victims of groupism, collectivism and mass-mindedness. But I also have files which reflect the lives of people who dared to be individuals, who dared to break away from established isms and who dared to combat negative and uninspiring social forces. These people are living magnets. They have made places for themselves by utilizing their power of belief and turning to their Selves.

SHE SAID: "I WAS JUST A BLOB UNTIL I STARTED USING THE MAGNETISM CREED."

Annie D. lives in Chicago, Illinois. Her greatest complaint was that nothing ever happened in her life. She felt that she was just one face among too many, a blob. Her problem is a prevalent one. She had become so embedded in the mass that she lost her individuality. The Magnetism Creed put her back in touch with her Self. She became a center of psychic gravity. People were attracted to her. New men came into her life. She got a new job, a new personality and a new outlook on life. She doesn't make any more money than before but she now has at her disposal many of the wonderful things of life which she desired.

HOW A JOBLESS DERELICT REGAINED HIS SELF-RESPECT

Ronald P., of Trenton, New Jersey, was down and almost out. He was a derelict or in his own words, "a stumbledown bum." Ronald started practicing the Magnetism Creed nightly and he began to have visions of how he used to be. This wasn't idle daydreaming; it was creative reverie. Ronald re-established his rightful connection with the Transcendent Cohesive Force which pulls everything in the universe together for ultimate good. He became a magnet for peace, joy, pleasure, personality and effectiveness. He stopped drinking, stopped lazing, stopped crying over spilled milk and he advanced steadily thereafter. Ronald is now making $700 a month, owns a new car, has plenty of girlfriends and is forward-looking. He laughs because some people think he's a bit touched in the head. He goes around murmuring: "I *believe* in Attraction: Cosmic drawing power . . ."

WHAT YOU DESIRE IS WHAT YOU BELIEVE

When you are overtired, you want rest. When you are sick, you desire health. When you are poor, you desire money. When you are overworked, you want relaxation. What you desire, you believe possible, otherwise you wouldn't desire it. Desire the good things of life, but desire with belief in their attainment. Go forth believing. Activate your power of belief, use the Magnetism Creed and get ready to receive from every direction, known and unknown. Don't be afraid to desire great things. The Unconscious knows no limitations.

15

How to Master Obstacles and Setbacks with the Victory Creed

The book of Ecclesiastes (9:11) states: "The race is not to the swift, nor the battle to the strong." And yet, how dismaying it is to see those stronger than we reaping a harvest of fulfillment while we suffer lack and difficulties. How discouraging it is when we hear of "swift" but dishonest men and women gaining in this life while we lose continuously. We begin to wonder, How can the Bible say that the race is not to the swift, nor the battle to the strong? Who then wins the race and conquers in the battle? The answer is paradoxical on the surface: the victor, the true victor, is he who neither fights hard nor runs fast, but he who knows that Victory in the physical world is a mirror of Mastery in the spiritual world. Put another way: a man can bully his way up the ladder of success and achieve empty victory, but the man who turns to the divine, the godhead, the Self, experiences glory in victory.

When you see, hear about, or read about thieves and murderers getting away with their crimes and apparently enjoying life, don't be misled. The media has a way of sensationalizing and distorting facts of life. You should be aware of that and ingest it accordingly. Moreover, you should know that true victory for any man comes from within.

If you have obstacles in your path to success and fulfillment, and you know in your heart that you cannot as a living, feeling human being, resort to criminal or nefarious deeds, you are then an initiate qualified to tap the inner source of wealth, happiness and success. If you are one of those rare spirits who does not believe in abuse of power, in persecution and in oppression, then you are a candidate for receiving higher-than-human aid and succor. You are one of the ones who can win without running with the pack or battling at the side of the aggressive. It is you who can activate the potent power of belief which resides within you to call into your life all the beauty, joy, and plenty you desire. The power of belief can remove any obstacles in your path, any difficulty in your life, and obstruction in the way of your success and happiness.

HOW A MAN CONQUERED HIS GREATEST ENEMY

Gordon U., a man I met during a stay in Topeka, Kansas, is what many call "a gentle person." Gordon has many friends; he is thoughtful, kind, and considerate of others. However, when I talked with Gordon, his greatest assets had become his biggest weaknesses. Gordon was being persecuted and undermined by a crude, unfeeling man at the company where both worked.

Gordon said: "I just can't combat this man on his terms. I haven't got what it takes. He's sly and underhanded. He steals from the company and makes more money than I do because of it. He's always buttering up to the bosses and he looks like a shining personality. They don't seem to recognize his true face, but I see it every day. He plots and connives and talks behind everyone's back. I know he has kept me from promotions dozens of times in the past few years. I don't know what he says or does, but he's effective. He keeps getting ahead, and I'm in the same position I was in when I started working. And I can't go to the bosses with this. It would sound so petty. I'd be like him! What am I going to do?''

The first thing I had to do was rebuke Gordon. I told him to stop underrating himself. I said, "How can you even consider yourself inferior? You don't plot; you don't connive; you don't undermine others—why you should be *proud* of yourself! Now get that worried, harried look off your face and listen . . .''

I explained to Gordon, slowly and carefully, that there isn't an enemy in the world who cannot be overcome if one knows how to go about overcoming. I told him there was no need for him to start exhibiting unsavory qualities or underhanded ways.

I said: "Sure, this man is winning by being clever and devious. So what? That has nothing to do with you. To each his own. What you have to do—and you have the spirit for it—is let Mastery come *through* you. This man is in your way, obstructing you, keeping you back, but you don't have to fight on his terms, with his weapons. Get in touch with Mastery and you will become victorious.''

I explained to Gordon that Mastery is a superhuman capacity, Victory its human counterpart. I said: "If you are going to be victorious, you have to get back in touch with the source of Victory. You must stop believing that this man is right in what he is doing, no matter how successful he appears. You must reactivate your own power of belief in true Mastery, a Transpersonal agency, get in touch with it, and permit it to flow through you into your physical life in the form of personal Victory.''

Once Gordon had renewed his faith in Victory and in the overcoming of obstacles and setbacks, he was ready to receive the Mastery Creed. He recited it every night orally and every day mentally, for about two weeks. This re-established his connection with Transcendent Mastery. He was in his third week of creed-recitation when the news came. His arch enemy had been caught stealing from the company. The man was fired. But that wasn't the end of the matter. Because the man had been caught stealing, the company owners thought it wise to give the books an audit. This investigation showed that huge amounts of money and merchandise had been pilfered over the months. The investigation resulted in the arrest and imprisonment of that man.

Gordon did not see any connection between his creed-recitation and the man's downfall. But one day Gordon was called into the main office, and to his complete surprise, a humbled and apologetic boss said: "Gordon, we owe you an apology. We believed N. to be a go-getter, and I'm afraid we believed the things he reported about you. Recent developments clearly show that we've been taken in, and we have lost thousands of dollars for our stupidity. Can you forgive us?"

Of course Gordon could do that. He's that kind of a man. Consequently, the boss said, "You've been with us for almost four years now and you haven't received a promotion or a pay-raise. And in all this time you have never complained, but have worked hard and steadily. In view of recent developments we have come to realize that you are actually one of our most trusted employees. Everyone likes you, you know your job, and you're fair. So we have decided to kill two birds with one stone. We will make up for our unfair treatment of you and we will reward you for your years of faithful service. As of tomorrow morning, you are the general manager of the whole company. When you go home this evening, chuck your lunch box and that work uniform. Come to work tomorrow in your best suit, shirt and tie. Miss L. will show you your new office."

THE CREED THAT SUBDUES ENMITY
AND OPPOSITION

Gordon said: "I can't believe what's happened to me! Without lifting a finger, my enemy is beaten, and I'm victorious! I can't begin to tell you how the Mastery Creed has helped me through this terrible ordeal.''

Here is the Mastery Creed that Gordon uses:

> I *believe* in Mastery the Supernatural Agency, Conqueror of obstacles and setbacks:
> *And* in Victory its human counterpart: which is ordained by the Higher Self, meant for struggling man: disclaimed by defeatists, was unremembered, unused, and unwanted: it left man vulnerable; in times of trouble the wise recalled it: it activated in their lives, and made real to them the Supernatural Agency of Mastery: from thence it shall invigorate the obstructed and the persecuted.
> I *believe* in Victory: the ascendancy of truth-seekers; the overcoming of difficulties and opposition: divine aid in time of need: the intervention of Supernatural Agency: and in Victory indomitable.
> *Amen*.

HOW TO LET THE MASTERY CREED WORK IN YOUR LIFE

One of the best times for reciting the Mastery Creed is just before falling to sleep, the time when the conscious mind is relaxing from its day's labor, and the unconscious mind is beginning to work. The Unconscious, the Self, these will understand and be receptive to the creed, for it is at such times that the ego is relaxing also and permitting the unseen world of Otherness to operate. Slip into the euphoric state between waking and sleeping and repeat a few lines of the creed.

If you have a personal problem or an enemy, or something is obstructing your path to success, you may say:

> I *believe* in Victory: the ascendancy of truth-seekers; the overcoming of difficulties and opposition: divine aid in time of

need: the intervention of Supernatural Agency: and in Victory indomitable.
Amen.

Speak these words with feeling and belief. You are talking to yourself (your Self), and the Self will respond in your daily life. It works miracles for others; it will work for you.

If at first you have a hard time remembering the words of the creed or creeds, don't let this deter you. The Self does not mind if you have a light on. Nor does It mind if you read from this book. Even reading to yourself (your Self) can be most edifying. The important thing is to let the recitation of the creed reactivate your power of belief in Divine Aid, higher-than-human ways to combat enemies, setbacks, obstacles and adverse conditions.

I WANT VICTORY!

In uttering this desire, do not permit the ways of the world to interfere with your reaching the goal. Look at your situation; weigh the pros and cons; pinpoint the enemy, be it man, circumstance or obstacle. Then turn it over to the Self as follows:

I *believe* in Victory: the ascendancy of truth-seekers; the overcoming of difficulties and opposition, etc. . . .
Amen.

Then drop off to sleep repeating, "Amen," for this word means "so be it," or as the witches of old said it, "so mote it be." In other words you are saying, "Let it be in my life. Let me be victorious. Let me overcome." In essence you have done this: you have spoken with the Self, you have reviewed the circumstances surrounding your lack of success, and then you turned it over to higher-than-human agencies to handle for you.

You can learn to do the same thing during waking hours. Pause in the midst of a busy day and remember the Self. Perhaps an image will come to your mind. No one knows what the Self looks like. It is unrepresentable. But there are various symbols of the Self which serve mankind. Jung, as I noted earlier, calls Christ the symbol of the Self. You can image that one if you wish. Universal Mind is another symbol. Certain cards in the Tarot deck—like the Lovers Card and the Judgement Card—depict a guiding angel overlooking the humans. These angels are symbols of the Guardian, the Overlooker, the Guide—the Self. Any symbol may be used just so long as you remember that you are in the presence of divinity.

Let Mastery filter through your being into your life. Recite the creed, activate your latent power of belief in overcoming any obstacle, and Victory will manifest for you. Many different people use the Mastery Creed for many different problems, but it always works for them. It can work for you, too.

HE SAID: "I LOVE HER SO MUCH THAT I'LL DO ANYTHING TO HAVE HER."

When Sam V., of Akron, Ohio, said this, he meant that he would lie, steal, cheat and fight to gain the affections of the girl he loved. But he didn't have to do anything of the sort. He *thought* he would have to because there was another man who was beguiling the girl, dazzling her with his superficial charm and flashy car. Sam began using the Mastery Creed, however, and where he had failed miserably to compete with the hero-type, he succeeded miraculously when he ceased competing. He restored his faith in Mastery the Supernatural Agency and permitted the Self to operate in his life. A strange series of events changed the complexion of the picture. The hero lost his high-paying job. Since he had habitually squandered his money for show anyway, he was broke. His flashy car was repossessed. He became an embittered, carping individual, a defeatist, and a complainer about everything around him. He even accused the girl of using him! She turned to Sam for help and love blossomed. In time, Sam was happy to hear her say: "You're so steady, Sam. I feel so secure when I'm near you." Sam emerged the victor in a fight he didn't even fight! The Self did it for him!

WHY THE SELF RESPONDS TO CREEDS

Sam learned a valuable lesson we all have to re-learn. The Self is always at work positively or negatively, depending upon our relation to it. Sam established a good and positive relation to It, and the Self responded accordingly. The hero, on the other hand, had no conception of the Self, but depended entirely on superficial agencies for his life. And the Self reacted accordingly. Remember this: there is a direct relationship between the events of life and the Self. The Self is behind every physical phenomenon. The Bible puts it this way: "I form the light, and create darkness: I make peace, and create evil: I the Lord do all these things." (Isaiah 45:7). Which way the Self (or God) will act in your life depends strictly upon your power of belief. Psychologically speaking, Sam's adversary had "repressed" the Self. When Unconscious contents are repressed by humans, they erupt at their own will, usually in adverse ways. We might say that "repressed" belief in good luck results in bad luck, that "repressed" belief in happiness results in sadness, and that "repressed" belief in Mastery results in total failure. Whereas belief in Mastery results in personal Victory. This is what happened in Sam's life. And it can happen in yours.

ECSTATIC EVENTS AND MERRY MIRACLES

The following are just a few cases from my files of people who have successfully used the Mastery Creed to reactivate their power of belief and to permit the Self into their lives.

Karen H., of Harrisburg, Pennsylvania, wanted more than anything else to be an editor of a leading magazine. She was qualified—a graduate of a famous women's college—but she was blocked at every turn by male chauvinism. She remained a mere worker in the company until she reactivated her belief in Supernatural Agency. One night while meditating on the Mastery Creed an intuition flooded her conscious mind. She followed through with it and today Karen is the owner-publisher of her *own* national magazine. The Self removed her obstacles by removing her from *them!*

Bill B. was walking along a Lincoln, Nebraska street one evening when he was accosted by a drunk. The intoxicated man was huge, a veritable blockhouse. Bill knew that the man was going to hurt him and he also knew he was trapped. Bill mentally called upon the Self, recited the last part of the Mastery Creed. At that very moment, the mean-tempered drunk swung a beefy arm to knock Bill down, but he slipped, or tripped, or stumbled, or something. The huge fist whistled past Bill's face; the big man fell in a heap at his feet, knocking his own head against the pavement. Bill heaved a great sigh of relief and walked away. People later reported that slightly-built Bill had done something magical to subdue his opponent!

Donna A. felt suffocated in the small town where she was raised. But there seemed no way to get out of her stifling trap. By getting back in touch with the source of Overcoming, Donna had her dream come true. She won a scholarship and was able to attend a college in a big city miles away. Donna writes that "this is paradise!"

ONE POWER INDIVISIBLE

The most valuable bit of knowledge you can possess is this: There is only one power in the universe. It is the power of belief. If you believe that setbacks can deter you, by God, they will! If you believe conditions are so bad that there is no possible way for you to overcome them, then you are on a one-way street to nowhere. If you believe people can hold you back, then they can. Now this says nothing about setbacks, conditions, and people, but it says everything about you. As you *believe* so it is to you. Analyze yourself and honestly ask: "How am I using my power of belief?" The answer which only you know will give you tremendous insight into your life. The Mastery Creed may be the very thing you need to rise above or to avert opposition. It can lead you to miraculous victory!

16

How the Immutability Creed Gives You Stability in the Midst of Chaos

Everywhere I go these days I meet people who are worried, uncertain of themselves, and even less certain about the age in which they live. Changing morals, shifting traditions, revolutions, and evolutions—all of these epochal phenomena leave them feeling alienated, unsteady and insecure. Change seems to be the order of the day, and change creates instability for many people.

HOW TO BE A ROCK OF GIBRALTAR

You need not become a victim of changing times. You need not feel like a helpless leaf in the wind. No, you can be a veritable Rock of Gibraltar. The key lies in your consciousness of the facts of life. Though you may be surrounded by change, you can know with certainty that behind it, in a strange and mysterious way, lies Order.

Change is a part of our heritage. From the shift from the Age of Aries to the Piscean Age, to the switch from the Industrial Age to the Space Age, change has been an integral part of human life. But down through the centuries of shifting times there have been select human beings who were not unsettled and uprooted by change. These special individuals had one thing in common: *belief* in Immutability the Essence of Order. They knew that beyond the appearance of fluctuation there lay organization. They *believed* in Order.

When you activate your power of belief in Order beyond Chaos, you bring into your life those qualities you require in order to survive in the midst of chaotic society. You can be the Rock of Gibraltar in the midst of clashing waves on a storm-tossed sea.

How?

By restoring your faith in Immutability.

THE CREED THAT GIVES YOU POWER TO SURVIVE

Here is the creed that will help you stabilize in the face of change, whether that change is physical, social, national, emotional, spiritual or psychic:

> I *believe* in Immutability the Essence of Order, Organizer of ebb and flow:
>
> *And* in Stability its external counterpart: which is underlying all phenomena, supporting all manifestation: denied by faulty reason, was challenged, disbelieved, and discredited: it seemed illusory; it establishes and sustains adherents: it supports believers, and sustains their lives with Immutability the Essence of Order: it continues to stabilize the wavering and the insecure.
>
> I *believe* in Stability: firm resolve; the solidity of faith: the error of uncertainty: the rewards of constancy: and in Immutability unshakeable.
>
> *Amen.*

HOW THE IMMUTABILITY CREED WORKS FOR YOU

When you reactivate your power of belief and affirm the reality of Order behind Chaos, you allow Immutability to imbue you with steadiness and infuse your life with constancy. Your power of belief alone can make you as steady as a rock while others around you waver, stagger, and even fall.

HOW THE IMMUTABILITY CREED
INCREASED A MAN'S SALARY

When technological progress came to the V. Manufacturing Company, Benjamin T. was as much at a loss as his fellow workers. Advances in machine design had radically changed the machinery and its operation. Men who were used to the old ways found it extremely difficult to adjust to new and faster methods. Every employee had to re-learn certain basic operations. This required time, and the company was losing money in the process. Since the employees are the backbone of any corporation, the company had no choice but to hope that the men would learn the new techniques quickly. But many men found it almost impossible to adjust. They stood around and scratched their heads and muttered under their breath about the disruptive aspects of technological progress. Some were unable to cope at all and quit their jobs in disgust.

Benjamin T., however, was already practicing the Immutability Creed. He, too, had to learn about the new changes in machinery and in their operation, but he did not falter like so many of the rest. He affirmed his belief in constancy and applied himself as he would to any task. Consequently, Benjamin became most adept at handling the new machines. Before this time, Benjamin was just a worker among workers, but his ability to remain steady and unflustered in the midst of chaos lifted him to fame and fortune. He was making $2.85 per hour at the time of the big change-over. When the employers, who were sorely distressed about time-waste and money-loss, saw that Benjamin could operate the new machinery better and faster than even their most dependable workers, they were forced to make him foreman. Overnight Benjamin became the lead foreman of the day shift, earning over $200 per week. He attributes his success to the Immutability Creed and says, "It has restored my faith in stability. I don't care what changes happen, I'm me and I'm *staying* me!"

SHE SAID: "MY NEW ATTITUDES WERE DESTROYING MY LOVE-LIFE."

I received this letter from a young woman in Baton Rouge, Louisiana, who has been practicing the creeds, but who also had a very personal problem:

Dear Mr. Laurence,
When you were here last March, I attended your lectures and learned to use the Immutability Creed. I want you to know how it has helped me.
Just before I attended your lectures I was immersed in Women's Liberation and Feminism. I was gratefully learning some rather interesting facts about Masculinity, like this:
"Men are superior to women on account of the qualities in which God has given them preeminence."—*The Koran*
"Such is the stupidity of woman's character that it is incumbent upon her, in every particular, to distrust herself and to obey her husband."—*Confucian Marriage Manual*
"In childhood, a woman must be subject to her father; in youth to her husband; when her husband is dead to her sons. A woman must never be free of subjugation."—*The Hindu Code of Manu, V*
"Among all savage beasts none is found so harmful as woman."—*St. John Chrysostom*
There are many more things like this in the literature I've been reading lately, and I am very happy to be learning them. But I found myself carrying over my new attitudes into my

personal relationships. My popularity among men decreased steadily the more I tried to put my new attitudes into daily practice. My thinking and feeling were highly colored by these new facts turning up in women's magazines and clubs. I discovered that I was actually alienating men!

I wouldn't have known it at all if it hadn't been for a man who decided to talk to me straight from the shoulder. In fact, it was he who took me to your lectures. He and I practiced the Immutability Creed together. It changed our lives. No, it gave us our lives *back*.

I still remain receptive to rediscovered historical and religious facts, but I no longer permit them to interfere with my love-life here and now. Thanks to the creed, new attitudes and strange traditions do not move me.

Mary Ann L.

HOW THE IMMUTABILITY CREED MAKES YOU THE FIRST WITH THE MOST

Mary Ann's letter sheds light on an important point to remember: you don't *resist* change; you benefit by it. You glean all the gold from new issues, attitudes, and data, but you do not permit them to interfere with your life. When you activate your power of belief in Stability and the Essence of Order sustains you, then you are able to digest any new information and still retain your own integrity. This is vital today, for far too many people fail to note the difference between valid new data and mere fad. When you are stable—and the Immutability Creed can help you to be that—then you can successfully separate the true from the false, the eternal from the ephemeral, the lasting from the temporary.

To resist change is to defeat oneself. Many new changes are available for our own benefit. The pioneering work of Dr. C. G. Jung, for instance, has made psychology more meaningful for us. Technological advances have put many new inventions at our disposal. One day we may have our homes heated by solar energy.

Breakthroughs in psychic manifestation have also enhanced our lives and made new information available to us: we may find Atlantis one of these days. No, change should not be resisted. But fads must be distinguished from reliable cultural changes.

SHE BELIEVED IN A FAD AND ALMOST STARVED TO DEATH

The September 9, 1974 issue of *Newsweek* provides a typical example of what can happen when a person gets caught up in a mere fad. This article, called "The Starvation Disease," reports that a girl named Janet decided, "like many of her classmates, that she was too fat. In fact, she weighed 135 pounds, only about 5 pounds more than the average for her height. Her parents were delighted when Janet decided to go on a diet and encouraged her determined pursuit of slenderness. But when Janet reached her proper weight, she went right on depriving herself of food, insisting that she was still much too fat. Eight months later she entered the hospital weighing 74 pounds, the pathetic victim of her own self-inflicted starvation."

Newsweek reports that "Janet's bizarre affliction is known as anorexia nervosa, an emotional disorder that already affects thousands of young women during the high-school and college years and appears to be increasing rapidly in both the U.S. and Great Britain."

Here we have a pitiable case of a young girl getting caught up in the diet fad. Dr. Hilde Bruch, a Houston psychiatrist, says that the illness is now curable. But in the past, about one in ten anorexics actually died of starvation.

THE CREED THAT CAN PROTECT YOU FROM ILLNESS AND DEATH

When you affirm your belief in Immutability the Essence of Order, Stability infuses your body, your mind, and your spirit. Yes, they may invent the pill that claims to cure all your ills, but you won't swallow it. Sure, there's a new diet for losing weight fast, but you won't use it. Why not? Because you stand firm on your own ground, capable of weighing pros and cons, able to distinguish between the true and the false. You will be certain, sure, constant, while others become statistics in hospital reports. You will benefit by the good changes occurring and you will avoid the faddish claims of money-hungry tyrants. When you are like the Rock of Gibraltar, you succeed, benefit and improve.

HOW TWO HOUSEWIVES HANDLED SUDDEN AND DISRUPTIVE CHANGE

Linda Y. and Nancy P., both of Winter Park, Florida, had a lot in common until recently. They each enjoyed living in lovely homes, side by side. They belonged to the same social clubs. Their husbands both worked in the aerospace industry. They were a lot like sisters.

One day a change occurred in their husbands' business. For the first time in their friendship, Linda and Nancy had a parting of the ways, created by this change. The aircraft company was laying off employees by the thousands. Highly qualified men with college degrees and even years of experience were being laid off. When the "ax" approached Linda's and Nancy's husbands, these men were at least offered a choice. They could either be laid off or move to another branch of the vast corporation in another state entirely. The women's reactions to this turn of events illustrates what I mean when I say that sometimes change can appear to be threatening.

Nancy absolutely refused to part with her home, environment, social status, and feeling of security. She nagged her husband constantly, complaining of moving, insisting that the children would be terribly upset and refusing to consider such a change of living. So her husband turned down the offer to transfer to another state. Nancy said: "I thought this was the wisest way to handle the situation. My husband is intelligent, highly qualified, and I believe he could easily get another position with a company here."

Linda, on the other hand, did not balk at change. She was practicing the Immutability Creed. She and her husband were steady, constant and reliable. They moved away within two weeks and Nancy's husband was installed in a new office, in a new area and in a new state, as Regional Manager. He makes $25,000 per year.

Nancy's husband? Linda sadly wrote: "He's still unemployed, even with all of his qualifications. They may lose their beautiful home. He was earning about $20,000 a year. Now he's drawing an unemployment check every week for about $75! Oh, I wish Nancy had encouraged him to come here!"

Some people resist change so much that they wind up cutting off their nose to spite their face. Linda has come to recognize change as practically essential to this age's standards. She herself remains steady, unmoving, even in the face of such changes. She does not believe in disruption. She believes in Immutability the Essence of Order, Organizer of ebb and flow. She affirms daily: "I *believe* in Stability . . ."

MAINTAIN YOUR BELIEF IN ORDER AND YOU TRANSCEND CHAOS

The pounding ocean waves do not move the sturdy lighthouse. Though the sea of life may become turbulent around you, maintain your belief in Immutability, and the coarse waves will not harm you.

Earth changes, but thy soul and God stand sure.
—Elizabeth Barrett Browning

Believe, if thou wilt, that mountains change their place, but believe not that man changes his nature.
—Mohammed

Life may change, but it may fly not;
Hope may vanish, but can die not;
Truth be veiled, but still it burneth;
Love repulsed,—but it returneth.
—Shelley

In this world of change, nought which comes stays, and nought which goes is lost.

—Mme. Swetchine

Without constancy, there is neither love, friendship, nor virtue in the world.

—Addison

17

How the Harmony Creed Preserves You from Strife and Discord

The preceding chapter is intimately linked with this chapter. Immutability implies Harmony. Unsteady people are not successful people. Many of my clients practice both the Immutability Creed and the Harmony Creed in order to bring luck, money, joy, and happiness into their lives. As the Immutability Creed protects you from the winds of change, so the Harmony Creed preserves you from strife and discord. It can help you to survive under stress and help you to perform your daily tasks with impunity even in the face of overwhelming obstacles and setbacks.

BELIEVING IN HARMONY EXPLODES DISTRESS

When you reaffirm your power of belief and restore your faith in Transcendent Harmony, no exterior changes, no matter how far-reaching, can upset you or deter you from your goal of success.

147

Too many people have lost their faith in Harmony. Everywhere they look they see only disruption, discord, and enmity. They have lost sight of the Manifestation of Cosmic Order, and consequently, order is not part of their lives. They fail to see the correlation between inner and outer, the fine balance between interior and exterior events and phenomena.

When you get back in touch with this fundamental state of equilibrium, you become a veritable pillar of might and power. While others are distressed, angered, lost, you remain steady, clear-headed and self-assured (Self-assured).

HOW THE HARMONY CREED HELPED
43 MEN AT ONCE

Frank R., of Wichita, Kansas, has this to say: "When I went to work for the P.L. Company I walked into a hornet's nest. Every man in the place was angry and at odds with every other man. The reason for their discontent was poor pay, bad working conditions, long hours and very few rewards. After about a week on the job, working under adverse conditions, bombarded by all this negativity, I decided to do something about it. After work one day, I gathered the 43 employees together. I told them we were all in the same boat, that we ought to quit fighting amongst ourselves. None of us, I told them, could afford to quit: we had families to support, food to buy, taxes to pay and houses to take care of. Let's work together, I said. Let's at least make the best of what we've got, instead of dragging ourselves down with anger and bitterness.

"Amazingly enough, every man listened to me. Encouraged by this turn of events, I wrote your Harmony Creed on a blackboard and told the men how I had been using it for months with remarkable results. I told them how it has helped me keep a level head even when things are so bad I want to get violent. They all responded positively and within a week we were all changed men. If you came to this company now you'd see laughing, singing workers—not because the company has helped us, but because we've helped ourselves. Conditions are the same. Bosses fight with one another. Fear and worry permeate the offices, but in the factory, we men are together, creating harmony in our own lives, no matter what's going on around us. This wonderful state of mind has spilled over into our private lives. We hold huge parties on weekends where all of us bring our wives and children. We're still underpaid, but life is a ball!''

SOME TESTIMONIALS FROM HARMONIOUS PEOPLE

I accumulate a great deal of correspondence from all over the states. Some of this mail contains problems and questions needing answers. Some of it reflects the results of creed-recitation. The following excerpts from letters come from the latter type of mail:

> The Harmony Creed saved me from becoming a bigoted enemy to fellow human beings. When some Puerto Ricans moved in next door I was furious with prejudice. I don't know why, except maybe it was from my upbringing. But these people didn't do anything wrong to me. In fact, they soon outshined a lot of my other neighbors. I was shocked at myself, for I didn't know I could be prejudiced. It was the Harmony Creed that reminded me daily that *all* people are my brothers. Now we and the new neighbors are quite friendly, living together in peace and quiet.
>
> Susan P.

> My wife left me six months ago. I lost my job right after that. My teenaged son was arrested for possession of marijuana. I was sick, alone and hopeless. I felt as if the whole world was against me. The changes happened too fast. I couldn't cope with the vast and rapid changes. I was losing control of my sanity. My nerves were frazzled. I thought I'd wind up in a mental hospital. But the Harmony Creed came to my rescue. It restored my faith in Cosmic Order, and reminded me that peace and tranquility do exist. I tapped the source of that peace and today

I'm back on my feet, working steadily, and enjoying my new life.

Cliff B.

When I was destitute and alone, nothing could help me. I want you to know that alcohol didn't help; carousing didn't help; lying to myself didn't help; cursing others didn't help. The only help I ever got was from the Harmony Creed. I *believe* in composure.

Victor C.

As a police officer I find the Harmony Creed highly instrumental in reconciling differences between some people. It helps me to help them and I don't have to arrest them.

Leo K.

THE CREED THAT ANNIHILATES
FEAR AND STRESS

What is this creed that so many people find effective in their lives? It is the Harmony Creed, as follows. Absorb every word, reactivate your power of belief in Peace beyond Discord. Affirm for yourself:

I *believe* in Harmony the Manifestation of Cosmic Order, the origin of peace and tranquility:

And in Equanimity its primary goal: which is designed for every man, originating in the Higher Self: disturbed by human error, was shunned, avoided, and lost: it retreated from man's life; in the day of great stress, it was missed: it was reactivated, and balances the lives of all who seek Harmony the Manifestation of Cosmic Order: for such it shall provide concord and unison.

I *believe* in Equanimity: inner and outer balance; peaceful coexistence: the danger of discord: the availability of composure: and in Harmony indefatigueable.

Amen.

HOW JFK SUED FOR PEACE AND HARMONY

Harmony is a rare commodity these days. People continually fight one another, if not over issues, then over property and jobs and loves. Some have battled because of differing views about the outcome of scientific and technological progress. When President John F. Kennedy was confronted by this obvious animosity, when he saw the fears of some people, and the doubts of others, he endeavored to restore their vision of harmony. In his 1961 Inaugural Address, President Kennedy said:

> Let both sides seek to invoke the wonders of science instead of its terrors. Together let us explore the stars, conquer the deserts, eradicate disease, tap the ocean depths, and encourage the arts and commerce.

In the same address, President Kennedy said: "Let both sides join in creating a new endeavor—not a new balance of power, but a new world of law, where the strong are just, the weak secure and the peace preserved."

There is no way of telling just how many hearts and minds this great president's words touched, but one thing is certain: the life of peace and harmony is available to anyone who wishes to achieve it.

HARMONY IS ITS OWN REWARD

When you get in touch with your own center, the Higher Self, from which all harmony proceeds, you can bring peace and harmony into your life even in the midst of chaos, disorder, enmity, strife and stress. Harmony is its own reward, for people who believe in Harmony reap rich rewards of peace, plenty and health. How? Think about it for just a moment. How can a man who is at odds with himself win in life? How can a group that is indecisive and combative ever hope to excel? How can anyone who believes that the world is falling apart expect to raise himself to a position of security and success? Impossible. Harmony precedes success in every endeavor. When you reactivate your power of belief and permit Harmony to flow through you, your life and your surroundings change for the better.

HE SAID: "SINCE I STARTED USING THE HARMONY CREED I'VE MADE OVER $50,000"

I first met Roy M. at one of my lectures in Greenville, North Carolina. Roy was a full-time dishwasher in a large restaurant and a part-time author of articles for magazines. He had had little success with his writing, selling no more than three articles in two years. That all changed for Roy when he started using the Harmony Creed in a most ingenious manner. Roy explains: "The creed gave me such a terrific sense of peace and tranquility that I kept using it as a means to induce a special state of mind. I discovered that by using the Harmony Creed as a *mantra* I could produce in myself a state of consciousness somewhere between waking and sleeping. When I am in this state, my mind floats free. I don't focus on any one thought. I use the creed for about 20 minutes each evening like this.

"After a while I found that certain images kept emerging from my Unconscious, like the Self was giving me ideas. I then found that I could take these ideas and put them into book form. Miracles began to happen. Within six months I had written three whole novels. Every one of them sold to the first publisher I mailed them to. I received advance royalties totaling something like $10,000. Add to this figure my royalties to date and you see why I'm flabbergasted! Since I started using the Harmony Creed I've made over $50,000!"

HOW THE HARMONY CREED PRODUCES
THE ALPHA STATE

I followed up Roy's letter because it interested me professionally. It became clear that Roy had hit upon a method of producing the Alpha State of consciousness, the state during which people can receive great intuitions from the Unconscious.

Brain waves are emitted in four frequencies—beta, alpha, theta and delta. The beta frequency is the highest rhythm, the frequency produced by our liveliest waking state. When we suspend organized analytic thinking and turn inward, we produce the alpha rhythm. The theta rhythm accompanies a near-unconscious state of mind, and delta rhythm occurs when we are sleeping.

The alpha rhythm is the one we need for receiving information from the Unconscious and Roy has demonstrated that the Harmony Creed helps him achieve this desired and desirable state of mind.

THE MANY USES OF THE HARMONY CREED

Roy's use of the Harmony Creed can be added to many others, some similar in nature. Raymond D., of Nashville, Tennessee, reports that he is "better able to assimilate what school courses teach." Dolores N., of Seattle, Washington, wrote: "I have more energy now that I practice the Harmony Creed. My mind is clearer and sharper." Arthur L., of Boston, Massachusetts, says: "My art work is more fluid and looser. The Harmony Creed puts me in touch with color, vivid pictures and wonderful ideas." And a young woman from Boise, Idaho, Jane T., said: "My boyfriend and I had this terrible problem that threatened to break us up. I worried and fretted over it until I found the Harmony Creed. Just reciting it for

three days solved the whole problem. The answer came from somewhere inside.''

LET THE HARMONY CREED HELP YOU

There seems to be no limit to the uses of the Harmony Creed.
Whatever your problem may be, let this creed get to work in your life.
Whether your problem is outside interference or internal confusion,
the Harmony Creed can put you back in touch with peace, tranquility
and balance. Once you have re-established your own equilibrium you
can see things change for the better in your daily life. *Believe* in
Harmony and permit the Higher Self to manifest in your life.

HOW A NEW YORK WOMAN DEVELOPED PSYCHIC
ABILITY AND SAVED HER OWN LIFE

There is nothing mysterious about psychic ability. It is a product of
Universal Mind, or of the Higher Self. Psychic ability can be de-
veloped just like any other talent. Sometimes when we contact our
Inner Selves we contact the source of psychic manifestation.

Mona R., of Albany, New York, made contact with her inner
reservoir of psychic power in a spectacular and noteworthy manner.
She had been practicing the Harmony Creed for weeks to ''calm my
mind and keep me steady.'' Mona uses the creed as she drives to
work each morning. It was during one of these diurnal drives that she
had her remarkable experience.

She said: ''I was driving the same streets I always drive, the same
ones I've driven hundreds of times. I know the avenues by heart and I
knew, as I passed the corners of M. and T. Streets that the next
intersection would be Avenue R. and L. Street. But suddenly, as I
was mentally reciting parts of the Harmony Creed, I had what I can
only describe as a vision. I saw the next intersection long before I was

actually upon it, as though I were stopped there for a red light. I blinked my eyes but the vision remained with me.

"Suddenly I saw a huge black car come speeding from the right, careening around the corner. In this fantastic vision that car smashed into mine, tore it to pieces, and sent us both crashing into other cars. There were horrible grinding noises, like metal against metal, and then the splintering of glass. I saw myself covered with blood and I knew that I was dying.

"Now, all of this happened in a flash, one wild vision from somewhere deep in my brain. As I actually approached the intersection a strange nagging feeling overcame me. It grew stronger and stronger as my car approached the light. Suddenly, on the spur of the moment, I turned into a parking space. I was breathless, perspiring and strangely tense. I stared through the windshield, and in the next few moments I was to witness a horrible re-enactment of my vision, only I wasn't in it.

"A huge black car came screeching around that corner and smashed head-on into a different car. Both went squealing into the wrong lane. Two other cars smashed into them. Metal crunched and glass shattered. I heard screams. Panicked and frightened, I ran from my car to the scene where many others were running. I elbowed my way up to the front and stared incredulously at one of the victims. It was a woman my age. Her hair was my color. Her car was the same make and model as mine. And she was covered with blood as I had been in my vision. And when the ambulance and police arrived, my heart stuck in my throat. A doctor said, 'Stand back, stand back.' He knelt down by the lady, felt for her pulse, and muttered, 'This woman is dead.'

"I am thoroughly convinced that the practice of the Harmony Creed put me in a state of receptivity so that I could foresee that disaster.

"I practice it faithfully now, not only because it saved my life, but I want to see if I can't develop psychic ability to such an extent that I can be in a position to help others with it. I mean, perhaps I could have saved that woman, too, if I had had more confidence in the vision."

WHAT THE HIGHER SELF HAS IN STORE FOR YOU

In *McCall's* magazine of January, 1974, there appeared an insightful article about the wondrous powers of the mind, by Julia Kagan. I would like to share some of her observations with you, observations which explain some of the possibilities open to people who can produce the right state of consciousness. Miss Kagan writes:

> ESP—extrasensory perception—encompasses all sorts of things that can't be explained by traditional logic: clairvoyance (seeing things or events that are actually impossible to see in the ordinary way); telepathy (reading another person's thoughts); precognition (knowing future events before they happen); psychokinesis (moving physical objects by force of will alone); and several even wilder manifestations.

There are untold abilities within your Unconscious. If you have any problem whatsoever; if you are being attacked psychically by negative-thinking people; if cultural change disturbs you; if the present age of chaotic manifestation unsettles you—then you need the Harmony Creed. Recite it often, orally or mentally, while your conscious mind considers the problem most distressing to you. Then wait for superhuman aid. In other words, by using the Harmony Creed in this manner, you are in effect turning over your problem to the Unconscious. You are permitting your power of belief in higher-than-human agencies to come to work in your sphere of existence. Get in touch with your inner Self, and anything can happen. The Harmony Creed can alter your state of consciousness. Constant and repetitive recitation amounts to meditation, and this kind of meditation leads to alpha states.

THEY DO REMARKABLE THINGS WITH ESP

Miss Kagan's article lists these ways that ESP is manifesting itself these days:

> Uri Geller, a young Israeli, gives performances on stage and TV in which he bends pieces of metal by concentrating hard and touching them lightly.
>
> Russian scientists report that they have observed a woman named Nelya Mikhailova move compasses, matches and plates on a table by force of will alone, though her efforts leave her drained and exhausted.
>
> Dr. Gertrude Schmeidler, professor of psychology at City College in New York, conducted an experiment in which another psychic named Ingo Swann changed the temperature of a very delicate thermometer sealed in a thermos bottle 25 feet away.

THE TELEPATHIC CHILD OF MRS. SKUTCH

Mrs. Skutch, Julia Kagan, reports, has a daughter who is psychic. "The child, at two, was answering questions before they were even asked. Now she sends her mother telepathic messages about things she forgot to bring to school."

We hear more and more of such phenomena lately, indicating an increase in psychic ability, parapsychological events and ESP. Scientific investigation adequately shows that all these so-called gifts are actually "natural" to man. The problem is that the source of these fantastic abilities lies untapped by many people.

Most people are too busy to be bothered with meditation, introspection and reverie, and yet, repeated demonstrations show that remarkable gifts result when people turn to the Unconscious. What is lacking is an easy-to-use technique for getting in touch with this inner center of psychic activity. The Harmony Creed is one such technique. Its repeated recitation can make you receptive to Unconscious proddings, intuitions and ideas.

HOW A YOUNG MAN DISCOVERED A HIDDEN TREASURE

John L., of Scranton, Pennsylvania, asked me for a creed which would help him to overcome insomnia. I gave him the Harmony Creed and instructed him to recite it softly and aloud every night before dropping off to sleep. He did so, and from the second night onwards, he slept fine. But the creed did more than cure his insomnia. John wrote:

> The first night I used the Harmony Creed I tossed and turned as usual. It didn't seem to be working. But the next night it worked like a charm. I was asleep before I got through the third recitation. I dreamed that I found a treasure.
>
> On the third night I recited the creed again, and again I fell asleep easily. But I dreamed the same dream. It was uncanny.
>
> The same thing happened on the fourth night. By this time I was more interested in the dream. Why would I be dreaming the same dream over and over?
>
> When I dreamed the same dream on the fifth night, I woke up before dawn. I lay in bed thinking about the dream, its contents, its location, everything. It was clear in my mind.
>
> The next day, my boss asked me to drive him to his home on the outskirts of town. I did so, and after I dropped him off, I decided to explore this area of the country. I had never been there before.
>
> I parked my car and took a walk. I don't know where I was. I was in some wooded area. All of a sudden I thought I was dreaming. I was standing between the very trees which had recurred in my dreams! I walked the ten paces as in my dream and there I found a very familiar rock. Suddenly animated, I struggled, strained and managed to move the boulder. My heart was bursting with excitement, for by then I was certain that I

would find exactly what my dream showed. And I did . . . a decaying leather case studded with and containing jewels.

That case was sold to a collector of antiquities for $7,500. The jewels in the case are reputed to be buried treasure of pirates known to have lurked in this area centuries ago. I sold every piece of jewelry I had, twenty-three pieces in all. I have never received less than $1,800 for a gem. And that means my treasure has given me more than $40,000. Actually, one piece, a huge emerald, brought in $7,000 alone, so between that and the leather case itself, I've received over $54,000!

HOW TO EXPERIENCE THE JOY OF FULFILLMENT AND SUCCESS

Many people claim that they cannot experience the joy of life any more. Well, you can. The very stuff of life lies in the Unconscious, the source of all life. Get in touch with your inner Self through the recitation of the creeds dotting this book. Gain access to the miracle-working power within you and expect miracles. Anticipate changes for the better in your life. Recite the Harmony Creed and watch disturbing, blocking influences dissipate before your very eyes. Evoke your power of belief and daily affirm, "I *believe* . . ."

Believe that the Unconscious, the Higher Self, can work wonders for you, and it will. I don't know you personally, nor am I aware of your circumstances, but I know this: you have at your disposal an untapped reservoir of power, ability, joy and success. Only you can tap it. Only you can overcome the things which keep you from it. The Harmony Creed may help you to do that. Recite it, *believing*.

18

How the Progress Creed Turns Your Misfortune into Opportunity

Many people today feel defeated, hemmed in by circumstances, restrained, persecuted, deterred from success, etc.; there seems to be a widespread and pervasive feeling that there is an invisible but effective barrier between them and what they want out of life.

THE DIFFERENCE BETWEEN COLLECTIVE PROGRESS AND INDIVIDUAL PROGRESS

You will experience and enjoy personal advances in life, love and success when you become aware of the sharp distinction between collective and individual progress. Collective progress can be manipulated by man; individual progress cannot. The latter is a gift from the Unconscious to *you*. No one can share, remove, or interfere with your personal progress—once you are on the move toward your goals and desires. The secret is to learn *not* to confuse your personal progress with collective progress in general. Collective progress can help you, but it can also hinder you. For example, progressive working methods in a company can put you out of a job. That's progress! But it is the illusory kind, the negative kind, and hopefully the impermanent kind. In *Progress and Poverty*, Henry George stated: "So long as all the increased wealth which modern progress brings, goes but to build up great fortunes, to increase luxury, and make sharper the contest between the House of Have and the House of Want, progress is not real and cannot be permanent."

LEARN THE DIFFERENCE AND MOVE
FORWARD TO VICTORY

Once we emerged from childhood and childish ideas we learned fast that many times success comes to groups, not to individuals. The individual has been swallowed up by the masses. Consequently, more and more people fail to plumb their own depths of being and have forgotten the true source of success, victory and ascendancy. It is within.

When you reactivate your power of belief in personal progress and reaffirm your own ability to excel, you automatically set in motion powerful unconscious processes which will come to your aid. The Unconscious is like a mighty god, a beneficent god, willing and eager to lift you up in life. This is the true meaning of so many myths and fairy tales of magical rings and hidden treasures. Aladdin's Lamp, for example, is a symbol of your own psyche. You rub it and a mighty genie emerges to do your bidding.

When you get back in touch with the source of your own individual life the Unconscious comes to your aid. Personal progress is yours as a gift, if you *believe* in progress and advance.

THE CREED THAT AWAKENS YOUR
SLEEPING GENIE

Many people have come to me with a common problem: the world is too big, power is centered in a few and progress is denied them. I tell them to get back in touch with their sleeping genie, to affirm the reality of personal progress, and to exercise their latent power of belief in advance.

Here is the Progress Creed which they use to help them reaffirm their own dormant powers:

> I *believe* in Progress the Divine Order, Equalizer of positive and negative:
>
> *And* in Advance its sole aim for man: which is a gift to humanity, originating in Cosmos: withheld from the faint-hearted, was restrained, harnessed, and bridled: it ceased to operate; the hopeful reclaim it: it reinforces lives with Progress the Divine Order: when affirmed it shall increase the obscure and the degraded.
>
> I *believe* in Advance: the true Order of Progress; the pattern of success: the elevation of man: the achievement of excellence: and in Progress uninterrupted.
>
> *Amen.*

HE WAS FAILING BECAUSE HE DIDN'T KNOW HE COULD SUCCEED

A few months ago while visiting in St. Paul, Minnesota, I talked to a young man who was suffering acute depression because he said there was no way for him to get ahead or increase his income. He believed that corporative structure, with its emphasis on group effort and its devaluation of individuality, was barring him from the better things in life.

I explained to him that he was misusing his own power of belief, that he was lending greater power to collective progress than it really deserved. I pointed out that the more he believed in the corporative body's ability to deter him, the less effective would be his own personal powers.

I explained to him that the true source of personal progress was within him and that he must immediately stop believing that it resides in a soulless corporation. The Unconscious is individual-oriented, not group-oriented: it operates through Man, not Company. I told him that when he himself got back in touch with his own center of power, nothing would be denied him.

He began to affirm, "I *believe* in Advance: the true Order of Progress; the pattern of success: the elevation of man: the achievement of excellence: and in Progress uninterrupted. *Amen.*"

I added, "Remember that corporations and conglomerates are only as good as the individuals who sustain them. The ultimate worth of a company is its employees. Do not equate *your* progress with company progress. The company progresses only *after* you do. If employees ceased to excel in their work every company would collapse. The big corporation *looks* like a great megalith, but do not let its bravado fool you or undermine your own individuality. You are essential to its life, the very heart of the organism."

Grasping the meaning of the above statements, he reaffirmed his own sense of worth. After about three weeks of sincere creed-recitation, he was promoted. It was only a mere step upward in the impersonal machine of corporative procedure, but it was a step in the right direction: up. The promotion came to him in the form of a cold memo from some unknown executive way up on the fifteenth floor, but still it proved that a man can move ahead even in the worst conditions. This young man no longer believed in corporative power, and consequently the corporation became his stepping stone to success. This is a very modern version of Jesus' statement, "Be ye in the world, but not of the world." This young man is *in* the corporation, but he is not *of* the corporation. He doesn't let it do his thinking. He doesn't let it make his decisions. He is an individual who knows his job and is proud of it. And he moves ahead. Progress is his.

HE THOUGHT HIS JOB WAS TOO INSIGNIFICANT

James L., of Little Rock, Arkansas, had a similar problem and he came to me for some advice.

He said, "I work in a huge company, but I'm stuck away in the factory part, back in a corner. My ID card looks impressive. So does the big name on my paychecks. But when people ask me what I do for this huge corporation I'm ashamed to admit that all I have to do is hook these two pieces of metal together. Eight hours a day, that's all I do, over and over again, hook two pieces of metal together. I don't think anyone in that company even knows me. How am I ever going to get ahead?''

Before I could answer his question I wanted to know more about those two pieces of metal. I asked James what purpose they served. He explained that they later become integral parts of an aircraft mechanism. I asked him what would happen if the two pieces of metal were connected improperly. James laughed.

He said, "That's happened a few times over the years. If they aren't linked just right they can cause a plane crash."

That was what I was waiting to hear, but I asked further, "Have you ever linked them incorrectly?"

James assured me he had not, and I said, "Then that is your key to personal progress."

James looked nonplussed and confused by this statement. I explained: "Every big corporation relies heavily on computers and statistics. You may only be a number to these mechanical monsters, but remember this: the computer is registering your work performance and this is what counts to the executives upstairs. If you continue to think of your job as insignificant you may make a mistake and create havoc in the company by connecting those pieces of metal incorrectly. But if you will stop and consider that this is your job, good or bad, and do your utmost to excel in it, you will eventually come out ahead, I know that sounds weird, but believe me, those computers don't miss a trick. Just remember that machines do not run men, men run machines. You can run this one. Apply yourself to your job, no matter how menial it seems. Do an exemplary job at linking those metal pieces together. Recite the Progress Creed as you work, believing in your own personal advance, and trust that you are dictating to the machine. You are telling that cold, mechanical object who you are, what you want, and when you want it. The machine in turn will repeat these things to your employers. No, not in words; in statistics. The profiteers *will* take note.''

James listened politely, but I could see that he still doubted my words. I smiled and reiterated my theory about working hard at one's job. I impressed upon him the importance of excelling even in his unglamorous occupation. Why? Here is a saying which is attributed to Emerson:

> If a man write a better book, preach a better sermon, or make
> a better mouse-trap than his neighbor, tho he build his house in
> the woods, the world will make a beaten path to his door.

James wasn't too sure he understood the meaning of Emerson's quote. I explained to him.

I said, ''When you do your job better than anyone else does it, even if you're tucked away in a dark corner of a huge corporation, success will come to *you;* you won't have to look for it outside yourself.''

I reminded James of the line in the Progress Creed which reads: I *believe* in the achievement of excellence. I told him to excel in his menial task. That was my advice to this young man worried about his future. This same young man wrote:

> Dear Mr. Laurence,
> I had been mentally reciting the Progress Creed for about a month when the darnedest thing happened. Some man in a flashy business suit (from upstairs, I guess) came to me one day and said, ''If you think you can handle this whole operation the way you handle that job, consider yourself promoted to foreman.''
> And just like that, I became the foreman of this section of the shop. I've never seen the man again. All I know is that my paychecks are a heck of a lot bigger!

INDEPENDENCE AND PROGRESS
GO HAND IN HAND

Escapism is not independence. Some people escape from reality by hiding themselves in the folds of corporate skirts. They cease using their innate powers and permit the Company to act as nurturer, provider and mother. They sell out independence for false security.

Rebellion is not independence. The radical and the bank robber may declare their independence of law and order, but they are hardly free. They are slaves.

Independence, true independence, results from the knowledge of man's relationship with the Higher Self. The Progress Creed indicates that you are independent to the degree that you tap and rely upon Unconscious forces.

When you reactivate your power of belief in Progress and reaffirm Advance and Achievement, you are truly independent, and this independence precedes personal progress. They go hand in hand and neither exists without the other.

HOW HE EMERGED TRIUMPHANT FROM
CORPORATE MATERIALISM

A young man who had what he described as a miserable job sought his independence and progress without any knowledge of the Higher Self. He fell victim to depressed states, bitterness and anger. His initial recitation of the Progress Creed saved him from total depression, but not before he yielded to temptation. Attacked by his negative emotions and immersed in a miasma of gloom, he stole some company funds. At the same time, he saw the need to re-establish his connection with the Higher Self. Catching a glimpse of what he should be, instead of what he was, he managed to call me.

I reassured him of the immediacy of aid from the Higher Self, which knows no limitations. As an individual, I told him, he was far superior to any outside influence. He reaffirmed his belief in Progress and restored his faith in himself as an individual. I encouraged him to realize the dominion of the Unconscious, the existence of Advance, and the achievement of excellence—all independent of external events and conditions.

Shortly after he had begun to recite the Progress Creed in earnest the young man felt the power from within bubbling up into his physical life. His negative emotions began to dissipate, like so much murky fog in the face of a cool, fresh breeze. He more fully realized his dependence, not on things and places, but on the Higher Self, the source of his very being.

He went forth stronger than ever, reliant now on superhuman agencies, secure in his renewed faith in himself. He was not really a thief, and he knew it. Acting on faith, willing to give up his job if it came to that, he made an appointment to see the head of the company. With chin high and spirit intact, he returned the money he had embezzled.

The employer was shocked. He asked the young man why he had stolen at all. The young man replied forthrightly that he had lost all hope of being promoted in this company and that he had foolishly believed he could get ahead by stealing.

The employer was so impressed by the young man's honesty and ability to face up to his weaknesses, that he entrusted him to work in the bookkeeping department. As it turned out, the company was losing a great deal of money because of pilfering and embezzlement—small sums which were adding up. By placing a young man who had the courage to admit dishonesty in a position of trust, the employer assured himself that money belonging to wage-earners would be safer. There was no actual proof about who was stealing, but the woman this young man replaced was a suspect. After her departure and after this young man was working on his new job, much of the thievery ceased. Consequently, the young man progressed amazingly fast, earning more and more raises and eventually greater promotions.

BECOME A SELF-STARTER

It is extremely important that you grasp one essential fact: the Higher Self contains a potential picture of you—not as you see yourself in the mirror every day—but as a whole, happy and successful individual. The Progress Creed, like all of the creeds in this book, is designed to bring you closer to your high potential. Reactivate your power of belief in Progress; reaffirm your faith in personal advancement; and you will become a self-starter (Self-starter). The creed acts like a hand on Aladdin's Lamp; it rubs and activates the Self and allows great and lasting aid to come through to help you. You will find your true self (true Self) hidden, but waiting to emerge and materialize. You will become a self-starter, an individual amidst the masses.

Edwin Hubbel Chapin once said, "We move too much in platoons; we march by sections: we do not live in our vital individuality enough; we are slaves to fashion, in mind and in heart, if not in our passions and appetites." Your reactivated power of belief will infuse you with the vital individuality which Chapin refers to. You will be able to turn every misfortune into fantastic opportunity when you permit the Higher Self (or God) to come through you into the physical world.

In *The Marquis of Lossie*, George Macdonald said, "The whole trouble is that we won't let God help us." It's the truth, and consequently, too many people suffer lack and deprivation, setbacks and obstacles to their success. They don't believe in God—or Self or Universal Mind—and they suffer accordingly. When you take the bull by the horns and consciously use your latent power of belief in Transcendent Aid, then that Divine Beneficence will appear in your daily life, no matter who you are, what you are, or what your circumstances. *Believe* it!

Once you find your own center of being, nothing will deter you from reaching your goals in life. As in the previous instances, you will become excellent in your particular field and by-pass any corporate or group interference. In the end you will proudly say, with Thoreau: "I would rather sit on a pumpkin, and have it all to myself, than to be crowded on a velvet cushion."

The secret is know yourself (your Self). Use the Progress Creed to enhance your power of belief and let superhuman agencies come to work for you. You will feel new strength of character in yourself, surging confidence, and a new pride in whatever you do.

THEY DIDN'T KNOW HOW GOOD HE WAS UNTIL HE SPOKE UP

Barry M., of New York City, used the Progress Creed first of all to re-establish his own sense of faith. He reactivated his power of belief with it and with other creeds which appear throughout this book. After a few weeks, he used the creed to restore his own faith in Progress uninterrupted. You see, Barry also had that terrible problem of feeling dwarfed by the immensity of corporate business. He works in the stock room of a leading manufacturing company, and though he has always had aspirations, he never did anything about them. He was just hoping that sooner or later someone in this vast organization would notice him and rescue him from oblivion. Well, life doesn't always work that way.

I explained to Barry that he would have to get back in touch with the Being who *will* rescue him from obscurity: the Higher Self. Barry was an apt pupil, a sincere young man bent on achieving some modicum of success in this life.

He said, "I'm darned good at my job. No hang-ups, no trouble. I work hard and the job gets done well. But anybody can do my job—unloading trucks, shipping packages, storing goods. I want more exacting work."

"Like what?" I asked Barry, curious to know what he had in his mind. He told me then that he was a very good typist and would very much like to graduate to office work.

I asked Barry: "Do your employers know that you can type?"

"No," he said. "I don't like to toot my own horn around the company. I mean, everything is so controlled and regulated that it just doesn't seem right for a man to go around boasting about his abilities."

I pulled Barry up short right there. "Boasting!" I said. "Nonsense! If you have an ability, then let your employers know about it. That's one of the major problems today. Men are afraid to speak up for themselves. You should be proud of your accomplishments and if they can get you a better job, better opportunities, or better pay, then by God, you ought to use them for that purpose. If you are going to get ahead in this world, you'd better start taking pride in your abilities and know-how."

I reminded Barry of the words of W.S. Gilbert:

> If you wish in this world to advance,
> Your merits you're bound to enhance;
>   You must stir it and stump it,
>   And blow your own trumpet,
> Or trust me, you haven't a chance.

Barry had used the Progress Creed to get back in touch with Divine Aid, but he was also preventing it from manifesting in his daily life. He changed all that by reaffirming his belief in himself. He recited the Progress Creed nightly, claiming as his own the gift to humanity from the Self, which is Advancement.

Infused with self-confidence, impelled by self-starting power, Barry wrote a letter to the employers. He has permitted me to share that letter with you, not that it should be copied, but so that you can get a general idea of how he brought himself out of the crowd and proclaimed his individuality. The letter reads:

Dear Sirs:

I have been one of your stockmen for over a year now. I enjoy the job very much, which I think shows in my performance of duties. I feel I have achieved a certain degree of excellence in this particular field and I trust that the company has benefited by my dedication.

Today, however, I feel it is time to revaluate my position. I wonder if the company is getting the best of my abilities. My employment record doesn't reflect it, but I have in the past year taken typing courses and some business education. I think the company should avail itself of these new abilities.

I believe in advancement, so I humbly request an opportunity to serve the company in a position of greater responsibility. I believe that the company would benefit immeasurably if I were given a position in the front offices where my new abilities can be best used.

Sincerely yours,

Barry M.

Barry achieved his goal on the very day that the head offices received his positive letter. Now Barry has his eyes on the office manager's position. And I think he will succeed in obtaining it. Barry believes in Progress. He believes in personal advancement. He believes he is an individual and not merely a number amongst numbers. He will succeed. As the French writer Victor Mirabeau put it years ago: "He will succeed; for he believes all he says."

HOW YOU CAN RISE ABOVE MISFORTUNE AND ADVERSITY

The Progress Creed links you with potent and effective inner power. Before retiring in the evening, recite the creed, mull over its words, *feel* its import. You will laugh at misfortune and adversity, social pressures, chaos, setbacks, hindrances, obstacles. You will emerge an individual, proud of your abilities, capable of using them. Let the Higher Self help your ego. Bow the knee of fear and trepidation and power will flow through you into the outer world. No matter what circumstances or conditions are prevailing against you, you can overcome them when you tap and channel supernatural inner forces.

Adversity introduces a man to himself.

—Anonymous

God brings men into deep waters, not to drown them, but to cleanse them.

—Aughey

Adversity has the effect of eliciting talents, which, in prosperous circumstances, would have lain dormant.

—Horace

Great men rejoice in adversity just as brave soldiers triumph in war.

—Seneca

Sweet are the uses of adversity;
Which like the toad, ugly and venomous,
Wears yet a precious jewel in his head.

—Shakespeare

The truly great and good, in affliction, bear a countenance more princely than they are wont; for it is the temper of the highest hearts, like the palm-tree, to strive most upwards when most burdened.

—Sir Philip Sidney

Have patience and endure; this unhappiness will one day be beneficial.

—Ovid

The lowest ebb is the turn of the tide.

—Longfellow

Little minds are tamed and subdued by misfortune; but great minds rise above it.

—Washington Irving

If hard times or corporate insensitivity or misfortune plague you and appear gigantic and overwhelming, then affirm: "I *believe* in Advance: the true Order of Progress; the pattern of success: the elevation of man: the achievement of excellence: and in Progress uninterrupted. *Amen.*"

And go forth conquering!

19

How the Abundance Creed Fills Your Pockets, Your Heart, and Your Life

When John F., of Springfield, Illinois, told me that personal satisfaction and contentment were beyond his reach because money was so tight in the world, I immediately corrected him on one essential point: his belief in dearth.

I said, "You mustn't let your present circumstances cloud your vision of the truth. I don't care what the economists say or how high prices are or how short your paycheck is—wealth abounds! There is no shortage of money in this country; there is a shortage of individuals who *believe* in Unlimited Supply of all earthly needs. Even as you lament your monetary crisis, money is flowing like honey over the land. The first thing you have to do is stop believing in lack and deprivation. Set your sights higher. Take your eyes away from poverty and need and reaffirm your belief in abundance, supply, contentment and satisfaction."

To help John break his chains of doubt, worry and self-defeating (Self-defeating) beliefs, I gave him the Abundance Creed to practice.

174

In no time at all John was revivified, forward-looking and hopeful. In this state of expectation John received an important letter from a lawyer in California. The letter summoned him to Los Angeles where, to his extreme delight, he found himself the sudden inheritor of over $60,000.

John wrote later: "I can't believe how much money there is around! I've never even seen this much money at once. I look at my checkbook every day to make sure I'm not dreaming. I went out yesterday and bought a brand new car. I'm purchasing my own home in Beverly Hills. I'm starting my own business. It's miraculous!"

PEOPLE WHO BELIEVE IN ABUNDANCE
NEVER SUFFER LACK

Is there a lack of money? For some, yes. For others, definitely not. In her Orlando, Florida *Sentinel Star* report, "Hollywood Returns to Luxury While Others Scrimp," journalist Marilyn Beck points out that "while the world worries about financial woes, Hollywood rejoices over its return to prosperity." Miss Beck goes on to say:

> While housewives in Toledo, Tokyo and Tel Aviv scrimp to save money for groceries, Filmland matrons concern themselves with securing the services of high-line catering firms that have more business than they can handle . . .
> "You hear so much talk of recession, but we haven't felt it around here," reports Ronald Clint, manager of Chasen's Restaurant.

According to Miss Beck's article, movie stars are enjoying abundance and plenty. She reports that Groucho Marx is redecorating his whole house, a job which usually costs $200,000. Miss Beck reports the fine living of some other stars:

> George Segal is remodeling and refurnishing his Beverly Hills estate. Rock Hudson has hired a decorator to create an

expensive new look to his bedroom suite. And Neil Diamond is redecorating his office and home simultaneously.

Recently, Miss Beck reports, Cher Bono celebrated her separation from Sonny Bono. "For $40,000 Cher was able to decorate a banquet hall of the Beverly Wilshire Hotel so that it looked like a circus tent, hired professional clowns and circus performers to entertain—and provided over 80 cases of Dom Perignon champagne for her guests."

Beverly Hills florist, Harry Finley, is probably the No. 1 supplier of party decorations for the Filmland circle. Mr. Finley says that orders for Christmas parties are up beyond those of last year. Miss Beck says: "And that doesn't include the order of one movie star for a $2,000 Christmas tree. It does include, however, party decorations budgeted at $125,000 for one of his clients, whose at-home bash will feature 300 flocked Christmas trees, a tennis court covered in thick white pile carpeting, and four snow machines to transform the Southern California estate into a winter wonderland."

Miss Beck has more to say: "Soaring interest rates didn't dissuade Telly Savalas from signing papers recently for a $750,000 home. The Rick Nelson family has just added on a $110,000 nursery wing to their San Fernando Valley house. And Helen Reddy and Jeff Wald took possession in October of a $600,000 Beverly Hills estate—to replace the $250,000 Beverly Hills estate they bought two years earlier."

What does it all mean? It means that there is plenty of money around. And it means that there are people who believe they can have it, enjoy it and spend it.

Does this mean that you should become a movie star in order to enjoy life? Not at all. No matter who you are or what your circumstances, you can bring abundance, enjoyment, satisfaction and contentment into your own life, when you *believe* that these things exist despite appearances to the contrary.

The following creed has many uses, whether you want to fill your pockets, your heart, your life, or all three. It puts you back in touch with abundance.

THE CREED THAT BRINGS RICHES, SATISFACTION AND CONTENTMENT

I *believe* in Abundance the Unlimited Supply, Rival of need and want:

And in Satisfaction its generous benefaction: which is offered freely, given openly: but was negated, refuted, and nullified: it was lost; in troubled times it flows anew: it waxes fruitful, and fills the life with Abundance the Unlimited Supply: it lies dormant and waits to bless the trusting and the loyal.

I *believe* in Satisfaction: complete contentment; prolific supply: the myth of dearth which withholds; the acquisition of needs: and in Abundance without end.

Amen.

THE ABUNDANCE CREED WORKED MIRACLES FOR HIM

A few months ago I talked with a man who was destitute, jobless, financially embarrassed, and despondent. He said, "The bills are stacking up, there's very little food in the house, and the kids are going hungry. I lost my job, the landlord wants two months' rent and my wife is getting sick."

In spite of his dilemma this man affirmed: "I *believe* in Satisfaction: complete contentment; prolific supply: the myth of dearth which withholds, etc." He practiced the Abundance Creed daily, as did his wife with him. The results were nothing short of miraculous.

I would like to be able to say that this man found another job, that his income was high, and that this family therefore overcame their destitution. But that isn't what happened. When you open the doors to the Higher Self, anything can happen. Here's what happened to this man.

The landlord, seeing this man's terrible position, had a change of heart. Rather than dunning him for money, he filed legal papers so he could deduct the rent as a charitable donation. This means that this family can live in the house rent-free for as long as they like.

After about a week of reciting the Abundance Creed, the utilities companies got together and, as a goodwill gesture (which afforded them some very profitable advertising), permitted this family to use the utilities free of charge.

Two local supermarkets donated cartons of food to the family, enough food to last them a month, food which would have cost him anywhere from $120 to $150.

He said, "How can this happen? Some women came by and gave boxes of clothes and toys to my children. Some man a hundred miles away wrote and said he'd heard of our plight. He sent me a check for $250. I don't understand it."

I said, "You don't have to understand it. Enjoy it. This is life at its fullest. You opened the channel to the Higher Self and It is responding in an immediate and effective way. You and your loved ones can get back on your feet. And things will get increasingly better. Just *believe.*"

HOW A MAN ACCRUED A HAREM FOR HIMSELF

I lectured on the creeds in Tulsa, Oklahoma and emphasized the Abundance Creed because many of the people were suffering lack and want. Afterwards, I moved on, as usual. I flew to Phoenix, Arizona and lectured there. Then it was on to San Francisco, California. There a letter caught up with me. It was from a William T., of Tulsa. He wrote:

> Dear Mr. Laurence,
> I took you at your word. I reactivated my power of belief. I reaffirmed my faith in Abundance. I challenged the Higher Self to provide me with what I wanted. And I think you should know that it works!

I wanted girls, Mr. Laurence. Yes, girls. I'm twenty years old, not bad looking, but I've never had as many girlfriends as I'd like to have. So I decided to put the Abundance Creed to the test.

I went to a local restaurant where a certain cute redhead works. She'd never give me a tumble. I ate in silence, mentally reciting the last part of the creed, and all the while I gazed at this lovely female. After finishing my meal, I left her a substantial tip, and paid my tab. I was still mentalizing the Abundance Creed. As I walked from the restaurant, a voice called to me. It was the redhead. She had just been getting off of work. She came up to me on the street and thanked me for tipping her so well. She said she wasn't accustomed to getting such nice tips. I told her she was welcome.

It worked so well that I tried it on a blond who works the switchboard where I work. It took a few days, but she finally dated me.

Then I tried it on the landlady's daughter. It worked again! Then again with the woman next door!

You should see my little black address book now. I feel like a sultan with a harem!

Gratefully yours,

William T.

Apparently, the Abundance Creed gives you whatever it is you want most!

HOW A HOUSEWIFE SUPPLEMENTED HER HUSBAND'S INCOME

Ellen C., of Pittsburgh, Pennsylvania, apparently used the Abundance Creed for similar purposes. She wrote me a letter and explained that her husband was suffering setbacks on the job. His pay was inadequate to meet their needs and he was worrying himself to death. She decided to do something to help him. She said that other wives in the neighborhood had begun doing things to help their

husbands, such as taking in ironing, selling needlework, etc. Ellen, however, was of a slightly different bent than most housewives.
    She wrote:

> Jack had left $25 with me for the light bill. Determined to end our streak of bad luck, I recited the Abundance Creed, waiting for some inspiration. It came in the form of a door-to-door salesman. We got to chatting and I squeezed from him the name of a local bookie.
>
> I was on that phone most of the afternoon, playing the horses! I've never done this before. But I took the newspaper, the way I've seen men do sometimes, and picked a horse. Then I called the bookie and placed ten dollars on the horse's nose. I did this with four races.
>
> I listened to the radio most of the afternoon, getting the race results. Imagine my surprise when my first chosen horse came in first, paying what's called 4-to-1.
>
> Every horse I bet on came in. A couple came in second, but I had bet them to place! By the end of the day my $25 had become over $346!
>
> I haven't told my husband about the races. I told a white lie and said I'd earned the money over a period of weeks by helping the neighbors out. I told this white lie because I wouldn't want him to think I'd get caught up in horseracing. I know how some people develop a terrible need for it, and I know a young lady shouldn't be doing such things, but I feel justified, because the money has come in so handy.
>
> The Abundance Creed is still helping us even though I'm staying away from bookies and racetracks.

EXERCISE YOUR POWER OF BELIEF
AND EXPECT ABUNDANCE

The Abundance Creed is designed to bring you Satisfaction. It does not prescribe what your abundance should be. As the previous cases show, you get what you want.

HOW TO TRIGGER SUCCESS BY UNLEASHING
YOUR POWER OF BELIEF

Your biggest setback in life is your misuse of the power of belief. You use it every day—you believe the sun will rise each morning; you believe you are you; you believe someone loves you, etc.—but if you do not use your power of belief to trigger success, abundance, and happiness, these things will escape you.

Believe in abundance when it seems furthest from you. *Believe* in plenty when you have nothing. *Believe* in success when it seems illusory. Be a dynamic illusionist! Practice the Abundance Creed every day and let the Higher Self know that you *believe*.

Below are additional case histories of people who used the Abundance Creed for profit and pleasure. Read them knowing that these people are just like you. You can do as they have done—*and more!*

HE BELIEVED HE WOULD BE IN NEED FOREVER

Bill A. habitually complained of his job, even though he felt that he could not change it midstream. Others around him were without work, so he forced himself to continue in work which he found boring, tiresome and uninspiring.

For these and many other reasons, Bill was victimized by negative thoughts of lack, need, want, and deprivation, and these thoughts in turn undermined his health, his attitude toward life, and his own self-concept (Self-concept).

I taught Bill the Abundance Creed. With this powerful affirmation on his mind day and night he transcended negativity. He discovered that he could work at his job with nothing short of a passion. New energies seemed to be at his disposal. He looked happier, brighter, more positive in outlook. And while he worked in a job which was still tasteless, his mind—freed from chains of self-pity—charged him with new and fantastic ideas.

Bill found himself thinking about an occupation which at that time was viewed with skepticism by experts. With his mind clear he realized that today's skeptic is tomorrow's believer. He pursued the orphan occupation in his spare time nightly, reciting the creed as he did so.

In just a few months, Bill was proficient in this strange occupation. He started "moonlighting," that is, working two jobs, his boring one and the new exciting one. In the evenings he helped neighbors with it, then strangers. Before he knew it, people were requesting his services. By the close of the year Bill saw that he had earned upwards of $15,000—and this in his *spare time*. Bill quit his first job and dedicated himself to the new one. He is now making over $20,000 a year, working from his own home, in his spare time. He is in such demand now that he does not have to worry about income. In fact, he is planning to cut his work load and spend two or three days a week just relaxing.

HOW JUNE P. TRANSFORMED HERSELF FROM A NAGGING HOUSEWIFE INTO A POWERFUL HELPMATE

June P. was as worried about prices and the cost of living as many other housewives, but she had a terrible habit of nagging her husband incessantly. "Why don't you work more overtime," she would cry. "Why don't you get a better job? The bills are piling up. The electric company is threatening to turn the lights off! Why don't you do something?"

The more June nagged, the more depressed her husband became and this was reflected in his work where he was growing less and less reliable. When June came to me for advice about how to get her husband to solve their problems, I told her that her problems would never be solved because she was acting on a false premise.

I said, "Your husband is not the key to the problem. He can't give you all the things you are asking for. He would have to be a superman to fulfill your wishes. And all the nagging and carping in the world isn't going to help. When you nag at him in this way you undermine his own sense of worth and you detract from his efficiency. What you want can only come *through* him, but the source is not him."

I taught June the Abundance Creed to put her in touch with the true source of all supply and abundance. In just days she ceased nagging her husband and waited to hear from the Higher Self. Her husband, liberated from her oppressive behavior, was able to think again, clearly and positively. He applied himself at work, actually whistling while working. His home life became happier. There was even a rekindling of lost love between him and June and they laughed and sang together.

June's husband came home one evening grinning from ear to ear. The company had just made him a traveling salesman for the products they manufactured. June and he were able to travel the country together, seeing all the wonderful things people with a lot of money get to see. With her new positivity, both she and her husband became happy, carefree individuals, moving in and out of the masses like invisible spirits, enjoying themselves, earning more money than ever before and loving one another. June had become a real helpmate to her husband and he considers himself one the luckiest men alive. Most of his monthly salary of $850 goes into their mutual enjoyment.

HOW THE ABUNDANCE CREED PRODUCES AMAZING PROFITS

The new riches of every kind that many people have gained through the practice of the Abundance Creed are nothing short of miraculous. With this creed in their minds and in their hearts they banished want and deprivation and accrued wealth, increased profits and achieved success. They used the Abundance Creed as a golden pathway to abundance and plenty, whatever their desire, and they did so effortlessly, without straining or memorizing or willing. Getting in touch with the Higher Self, the Source of all Abundance, they permitted riches to *flow* into their lives. They stopped believing in dearth, want, need, regardless of outward appearances, and they went *inside*, in their spare time, at their leisure, and the genie-like power of the Unconscious worked *for* them. The Abundance Creed is truly a miracle-working wonder and you can use it profitably *easily*. Just *believe*.

20

How to Use the Creeds for a Lifetime Plan of Health, Wealth, Power and Success

Here, creed-by-creed, is how to use the magic of your power of belief in everyday life to combat all life-defeating agencies and how to acquire for yourself all the riches, happiness, and success you have ever wanted—*without using a muscle.*

HOW TO REACTIVATE YOUR POWER OF BELIEF TO EMPOWER YOURSELF

If you feel like a "leaf in the wind," get in touch with your own inner storehouse of power and personal dynamism by reciting the Apostle's Creed with feeling and intent. In this modern day and age of materialism you need to know that deep within your psyche lies a wellspring of hope and help. The Apostle's Creed will help you to awaken your forgotten or ill-used power of belief so that it can come to work for you in your everyday life. Remember that "Amen" means "so be it." By reciting the Apostle's Creed orally or mentally you reaffirm your own *power of belief* and not the contents or meaning of the creed.

> If you believe the world is too big for you,
> If you believe materialism is squelching you,
> If you believe the "little guy" doesn't stand a chance,
> If you believe you will never get ahead,
> If you believe power is meant only for the rich,
> If you believe there are thousands of obstacles in your path to success,
>
> STOP!

Reclaim your right to the power of belief. Activate it by reciting, practicing and embracing the Apostle's Creed. Re-learn how to *believe*. Belief is a mighty power, and it is yours for the asking.

HOW TO OVERCOME THE MODERN OBSTACLES TO PEACE AND PLENTY

Modern industrialism and technology have wrought many miracles for you and me, but they have also undermined our sense of individuality and faith in life itself. If you sometimes feel that Mother Nature is being destroyed and with her all your opportunities for advancement, then recite the Universal Mind Creed daily and re-establish your belief in the inexorable power of nature and life.

If you think man has become a mere digit in a giant computer; if you think you are being dwarfed by the immensity of progress; if you think you don't stand a chance of getting what you want out of life; if you think there is no source of aid in these modern times—then use the Universal Mind Creed to reactivate your power of belief in the Eternal Source of all Good and permit the good things of life to *come to you*.

HOW TO CHANGE YOUR DULL AND DRAB
LIFE INTO ONE OF GLORY

When others make you feel inadequate, weak, or impotent;
When a loved one demands more of you than is justified;
When you feel that there is no one in the whole world to help you;
When you believe the contest of life is between only you and the rest of the world;
When obstacles and setbacks seem insurmountable.

That is the time for you to reactivate your power of belief and recite the Higher Self Creed. Like many others before you, you can tap this inner genie and without lifting a finger, you can enjoy a new and glory-filled life.

Recite the Higher Self Creed and *know* in faith that there is help for you, no matter what your cimcumstances, condition, or occupation. You don't have to do a thing except *believe*, and the Higher Self will appear in miraculous ways in every facet of your life, inner and outer, material and immaterial. Get in touch with this powerhouse within you by practicing the Higher Self Creed and you will begin to walk through life with your head held high and your spirits soaring while all around you others continue to wallow in the mire of defeatism.

HOW TO KNOW JOY AND HAPPINESS WHILE
OTHERS SUFFER FEAR AND ANXIETY

The powerful Joy Creed is your key to happiness when

Anxiety states threaten to enervate you;
Depression comes on through worry or fear for yourself and loved ones;
Life's inequities undermine you, hold you back, deter you from joyful success;
The world seems joyless and loveless and the mere need to face another day leaves a bad taste in your mouth;

You are unemployed, embittered, crushed by oppression, intimidated by high prices, devoid of gladness;

Hard work and dedication to duty sap you of vital energy and
deprive you of the good things in life;

The state of the nation's economy suffocates you as a person;

Another day seems like just another "drag";

You seem to be immersed in and surrounded by poverty, want,
need, and deprivation;

You don't believe money is looking for *you*.

HOW TO BENEFIT FROM MIRACLES WHEN OTHERS DON'T BELIEVE IN THEM

Your reactivated power of belief will create miracles in your life,
the kind of miracles that used to occur often, before mankind became
immersed in exterior, physical, and purely material beliefs. You
don't have to be like the rationalists, with their emphasis on intellect
alone, or like the technocrats, with their undying faith in machines.
You will emerge from the common lot of mankind and claim the
power of belief as your own and let it work in your life *for* you. How?

By reciting with feeling the Truth Creed, which puts you back in
touch with the Foundation of Life, Adversary to ignorance and
prideful intelligence.

The key to personal power in this life is not great intelligence nor
"inside" information nor aggressiveness. The key lies within you, in
the Higher Self, which is ready, willing and able to come to your aid
and lift you out of the miasma of gloom which attacks so many people
today. The Truth Creed links you with this inner dynamo and raises
you high above the common man.

The Truth Creed will help you to make renewed contact with your
power-roots, even after heartbreak and defeat. If you have suffered in
any way—on the job, at home, among acquaintances, in your love-
life—the Truth Creed will be a balm to your wounds and strengthen
you and uplift you so that you will become a strong, personable
and successful individual.

When external appearances fool you, when others seem luckier than you, when you are not being fully appreciated by others, use the Truth Creed to overcome all opposition.

When your job is joyless, boring, exacting, and you reap few rewards for your labor—use the Truth Creed and *expect* miracles!

HOW TO BECOME THE LUCKIEST PERSON IN THE WORLD

Luck is not mere chance; it is a powerful *force*. It is a latent force residing in the Unconscious, and the power of belief taps this source of good fortune and permits it to appear in your daily life. But you have to *believe* in order to *receive*,

> If you want the Midas touch.
> If you want others to befriend you and some to love you without reservation.
> If you want to tap the enriching power lying within you.
> If you wish to excel where others fail.
> If you want plenty while others suffer lack.
> If you want your ideas to pay off.
> If you wish to be rich, handsome and personable.
> If you would like to be known as a dynamic person.
> If you want to be able to reap rich rewards for your labor and energy-output.
> If you want to be freed from reliance on others.
> If you want to be admired.
> If you want the good things of life without selling your soul for them.

Then the Good Fortune Creed will help you the most. Recite this creed nightly before going to sleep and daily in your head. Let your power of belief awaken the dormant powers of good luck and you will begin to realize your every dream, wish and desire. Your power of belief is sufficient unto you, capable of putting you in touch with miraculous good fortune.

HOW TO MAKE OTHERS LOVE YOU, HELP YOU, SUPPORT YOU AND SUSTAIN YOU

The Love Creed should be used when you need the aid of other people. It not only makes others want to help you, it also makes you available to those who are *looking* for someone to help. Here is what the Love Creed can do for you:

It can make an enemy come to your aid when you most need help.
It can preserve you from the cut-throat behavior of others.
It can make you highly attractive to the opposite sex.
It can tear down the walls that separate you from happiness.
It can make even strangers like you, be interested in you and helpful to you.
It can change you from a statistic to a human being.
It can put you where the money is.
It can miraculously change your thin wallet into a fat wadded billfold.
It can relieve your depression, nervousness and lack of confidence.
It can bring you love, peace, harmony, aid, friendship, companionship and exciting personal relationships.

HOW TO BE A SUPERMAN AMONG WEAKLINGS

The potent Self-Confidence Creed builds a dynamic personality for you. Through its steady and faithful use, you will:

Achieve personality, character and charisma.
Become a living channel of vigor, spirit, zest and magnetism.
Be more personable and therefore more successful in whatever you undertake, be it work, play, friendship, love, or service to others.
Be more admired by friends and foes alike.
See a new person when you look in the mirror, speak to others and appear in public.

Gain enthusiasm, energy and vitality.
Permit Greater-than-I powers to permeate your life and benefit
by them.

HOW TO GAIN SECRET IMMUNIZATION
AGAINST SICKNESS AND DISEASE

If you feel rundown, listless and enervated.
If you want relief from nagging worries and pain.
If you wish health for others.
If you need help fast.
If you want more vim and vigor in your life.
If you wish to relieve suffering in yourself and in others.
If you want to overcome nagging aches and pains.
If you wish to dispense with constant irritations.
If you want toned muscles, healthy skin, shining hair and
sparkling eyes.
If you want wholeness, verve and dynamism.
If you want to tap the secret and powerful goldmine of health,
good vision, body-tone, glamorous stature and eye-catching
posture.

Then the Health Creed is for you. If you want to learn the secret to
sustained health and vitality, recite the Health Creed with feeling
nightly before going to sleep. This permits the potent Unconscious to
come through you and to bring into your life the strength and verve
you most need.

HOW TO BE SUCCESSFUL AND HAPPY EVEN
WHEN OTHERS ARE NOT

Turn to the Success Creed on page 74 when you:

Are depressed by "tight money."
Are oppressed by the high cost of living.
Want to emerge from depressed conditions.
Want a fuller, richer life in the midst of want.

Believe the economic situation precludes any success for you.

Are in despair of reaching your goals.

Want to explode impoverishment and lack in a magical and miraculous manner.

Are being denied the joy of accomplishment.

Suffer a drawn face, sunken heart, and defeatist attitudes.

Want your own personal success to be interminable.

Need an increase in income.

Are being dunned to pay bills you cannot meet.

Want to see your average luck turned into phenomenal good fortune.

Would like to see dollars, dollars, dollars, pouring into your life.

Are undermined in confidence by the negativity of others.

Wish to see your deepest desires fulfilled in this life, here and now, *for nothing*.

HOW TO BE MAGICALLY IMPERVIOUS TO OPPOSITION AND PSYCHIC ATTACK

When you reactivate your power of belief in Transcendent Help and use the Energy Creed to infuse yourself with power and endurance, secret miracle-powers of the Unconscious come to your aid. Here is what you can expect of the Energy Creed:

Freedom from psychological manipulation and the power to offset psychic bombardment.

Control over enervating diseases, situations and parasitic people.

The ability to regulate your will and strength when and where you choose.

The miracle-working infusion of Unconscious energy, vitality and enthusiasm.

Superhuman potency above and beyond that available to the average person.

Dynamic energy at your disposal, ready for use in work, love and play.

A new you as you conquer impotence, listless and poverty of
    strength.

The key to limitless power and non-depleting personal vigor.

The ability to turn deficits into surprising assets.

Cosmic Force which infuses you with creative ideas, vigorous
    spirit and dynamic self-direction which combine to make you
    forceful, admirable and personally happy.

HOW TO GAIN RICHES THROUGH
NON-PHYSICAL MEANS

When you affirm the Sustenance Creed you exercise your power of
belief in the infinite storehouse of riches which resides in the Unconscious. This divine source of abundant supply overflows into your
daily life to the degree that you permit it to, to the degree that you
believe in its ability to do so. In order to *receive*, you must *believe*.

When should you use the miracle-working Sustenance Creed?

When the good things of life seem too expensive for you.

When you wish you had more out of life—dollars, cars,
    women, clothes, furniture, shoes, fun, pleasure and excite-
    ment.

When you believe that lack is the fact of life.

When your income is inadequate to meet your needs.

When you want circumstances improved.

When you want to see your riches multiplied.

When you would like to see divine support come into your life to
    help you to help yourself.

When you want to see one dollar turned into ten, ten dollars into
    a hundred and a hundred dollars into a thousand.

When you want to see people, things, events, and circumstances
    come miraculously to your aid.

When you want to be lifted up out of the mire of want and
    deprivation through the magical agency of "meaningful
    coincidence."

When you are tired of inconsequential handouts, meager pay or
    insufficient funds.

When you want what is best for you, without effort, conniving
   or duplicity.
When you want all of your needs met, not just nominally, but
   fantastically, completely, and satisfyingly.

HOW TO GAIN RESPECT, LOVE, AND
ADMIRATION FROM OTHERS

If you want people to like you, to befriend you, to respect you;
If you want the opposite sex to look up to you, admire you,
   dream only of you;
If you want even strangers to sit up and take notice of you;
If you truly want to be successful, charming, and attractive;

   Then the Purity Creed is your answer to loneliness, lovelessness
and friendlessness.

If you wish to impress an employer,
If you want a woman or a man to fall in love with you,
If you want personality, charm, character,
If you want your own spouse to take renewed interest in you,
If you want wealthy people to *want* to help you,
If you want your ideas to be accepted and cherished,
If you want to dazzle people and make them pursue you,
If you want popularity, esteem and the joy of love,

   Then the Purity Creed is your key to magic elevation and fantastic
popularity. Overnight you can become the rage. You will find yourself admired, pursued and wanted, when you reactivate your power
of belief in transcendent qualities. Through the use of the Purity
Creed you will tap these qualities and they will emerge from within to
shine forth on your face, in your eyes, in your bearing and people all
around you will begin to notice the change and they will be drawn to
you.

HOW TO RISE ABOVE MEDIOCRITY AND
EMERGE AS A POWER

When you want to be a potent force in your environment and influential with people around you, practice the miraculous Cosmic Power Creed. Individuality, originality and specialness will mark you as a person of great influence.

You do not have to share the fate of the person who is regarded as unimportant. You do not have to be a mere statistic among millions of other statistics. You do not have to be swallowed up by the monster called collectivism. By using the Cosmic Power Creed daily you will infuse yourself with personal power and emanating influence.

When you are the one with personality, influence, forcefulness of character, energy, vitality and originality, it will be you who is called upon to fill the thousands of lucrative and glamorous positions available. You will get back in touch with the true source of personal influence when you reactivate your power of belief and recite daily the Cosmic Power Creed.

Hopelessness and impotence need not be your hallmarks. The Cosmic Power Creed will imbue you with untold quantities of vitality and untapped qualities like get-up-and-go, verve, importance and interest.

If you are tired of being attacked by the petty remarks of others who think they are better than you, then energize yourself by using the Cosmic Power Creed. You will emerge an individual, strong and undefeatable, and a worthy opponent of such backbiters.

If you *believe* in Cosmic Power the Ultimate Force, Devastator of impotence and weakness, then you will win where you once lost, excel where you once fell short, shine where you once looked foolish and gain respect where you once elicited mockery.

Use the Cosmic Power Creed to overcome ridicule, attacks on

your reputation and undermining false reports. You will emerge victorious in whatever you undertake.

HOW TO DON THE ARMOR THAT REPELS NEGATIVITY

Affirm and practice diligently the Guardianship Creed when:

>Someone who dislikes you is trying to ruin your life.
>
>Insidious remarks interfere with your progress.
>
>Your psychic atmosphere is polluted with the dangerous psychic waves of negative people who are greedy, violent, jealous, envious, hateful or repugnant.
>
>You are being bombarded by the virulent emotions and feelings of unlikable people.
>
>Negative energy is depressing you or making you angry, fitful or miserable.
>
>You are immersed in enervating atmosphere caused either deliberately or accidentally.
>
>You must deal with a particularly obnoxious person.
>
>You must undertake an odious task.
>
>Defeatist attitudes, negative traits, or less than desirable characteristics impinge upon your psychic space.
>
>You want an invisible barrier around you to protect you, guard you and keep you safe from harm.
>
>You want no longer to be the vanquished but the victorious.

HOW TO BECOME A MAGNET FOR MONEY, POSSESSIONS AND RICHES

You will be a shining light in the midst of darkness when you reactivate your power of belief in Transcendent Goodness, the Source of All. If you suffer lack, deprivation and shortage of finances, here is what the Magnetism Creed will do for you:

1. You will cease to despair of your dreams and begin to realize them in forceful and amazing ways.

2. No longer will your eyes be sad or your spirit wasted, for you will be uplifted, inspired and experiencing new joy.

3. You will begin to experience new and surprising joys of wealth as you continue to tap the source of transpersonal funds of abundance and plenty.

4. You will draw from the vast and overflowing storehouse of wealth and prosperity.

5. People with money and power will be drawn to you like iron filings to the magnet.

6. Whatever you want will be yours, be it a car, a house, a girl, a man, a job or anything you desire and *believe* is yours.

7. Emptiness and boredom will be strangers to you as your daily life fills with excitement, happiness, and contentment.

8. Your life will suddenly and miraculously fill with positive people, helpful friends and enamored admirers.

9. Nothing will deter you from success or hinder your progress, not joblessness, poverty, setbacks or adverse circumstances. Magic will enhance your life.

10. You will find that what you desire is yours, coming from every direction, known and unknown, lighting your every thought, word and deed.

HOW TO ACTIVATE A SUPERNATURAL
HELPER IN TIMES OF DISTRESS

If you are one of the many people who are suffering because less honest people are excelling in life and getting ahead—then come out of that crowd and achieve individuality and supremacy. You will overcome *any* setbacks when you use the Victory Creed and infuse it with your magical power of belief.

While others have to bully their way up the ladder of success, you will soar to the heights on the wings of your creed.

If you do not believe in abuse of power, persecution and oppression, then you will receive higher-than-human aid when you use the Victory Creed.

Let others plot, connive and undermine fellow human beings —you forge ahead constant in your belief that Transcendent Agencies are working for you.

Be a consistent winner with the Victory Creed. You will cut through obstacles like lightning through trees.

If you want to subdue enemies and negative people, recite the Victory Creed mentally and permit supernatural help to flow through you to conquer them.

If you want the miracle-working Higher Self to manifest in your daily life, recite the Victory Creed nightly.

To the degree that you use your latent power of belief to charge the Victory Creed, to that degree are you the sole possessor of great innate power.

To transcend the petty differences of society and the individual-defeating ways of the world, practice the Victory Creed with *belief* and banish all interference which prevents you from meeting your goals.

Use the Victory Creed when:

> You want to win the heart of a loved one.
> You want a promotion in your work.
> You want to overcome a bully.
> You want to better your lot in life.
> Someone else bars your way to love, liberty and the pursuit of happiness.
> Something blocks you from realizing your dreams.
> You want to reign victorious, strong, impervious and supreme.

HOW TO FREE YOURSELF FROM UNCERTAINTY AND INSECURITY EASILY

> If cultural and social changes, so swift and disrupting, are creating havoc in your life,
> If shifting traditions leave you feeling helpless,

If revolutions and evolutions render you ineffective,
If you feel alienated, unsteady and insecure,
If you are cowed by the might of others,
If you are victimized by the pushiness of others,
If you find it difficult to make a decision and then stick with it,
If inconstancy is your greatest weakness,
If conditions and circumstances overwhelm you,
If the magnitude of technological progress leaves you feeling
   dwarfed,
If new issues, attitudes and data confound you,
If you feel you must resist change,
If fads and overnight cures trick you,
If you feel you are surrounded by confusion and instability,
If fickle hearts and false promises dismay you,

Then start practicing the Immutability Creed immediately and see immediate results in your life, without your doing anything else but using your own latent power of belief. The ebb and flow, flux and change of modern life need not ruin you or dishearten you, for the Immutability Creed is your key to the very Essence of Order, Organizer of ebb and flow. You will withstand any barrage of change just as the mighty oak withstands the buffeting of giant storms.

HOW TO EMERGE FROM STRIFE AND DISCORD UNSCATHED QUICKLY AND EFFORTLESSLY

Put your power of belief to work for you. Use the Harmony Creed daily or nightly and you will:

Achieve the steadiness of character which marks all successful
   people.
Bring luck, money and happiness into your life.
Be protected from the winds of change.
Maintain miraculously under the stress and strain of daily liv-
   ing.
Perform your tasks and chores with magical alacrity.

Explode distress before it can overwhelm you and ruin your day
or your life.

Annihilate depression in yourself and in those you love.

Overcome the discontent caused by poor pay, long hours and
bad working conditions.

Burst from the bonds of prejudice, bias and favoritism.

Shine like a beacon even in the midst of dark, depressing and
soul-squelching conditions.

Rise above destitution and loneliness.

Become a mighty force in the lives of others.

Be respected as a calm and cool individual.

You will dominate over chaos, disorder, enmity, strife and
stress.

You will be imperturbable in the face of great odds.

You will achieve harmony, balance and equilibrium, and be
looked up to for support and guidance.

HOW TO ENJOY OPPORTUNITIES EVEN
WHEN OTHERS ARE SUFFERING MISFORTUNE

If you ever feel as if there is some invisible and indescribable
barrier between you and the good things of life, you can demolish that
blockage with the potent Progress Creed, the dynamic system of
getting ahead in times of trouble.

Read, recite and *believe* the Progress Creed on page 162 when:

You feel defeated, hemmed in by circumstances, restrained
from success, persecuted by others and deterred from reaching your goals.

Your own personal progress is blocked by collective progress.

You want to enjoy personal advances in life.

You wish to know love and happiness.

You want to know the secret to lasting progress.

The world seems too big and overpowering.

You want some of the power which is often centered in the select
few.

You wish to awaken the sleeping genie inside you who will do
your bidding.

Your own advancement is being blocked, undermined, thwarted, or in any way impeded.

You feel like a minor point in the vastness of huge corporate business.

You lose interest in your job and believe it is insignificant.

Triumph in life would taste the sweetest.

You need to be a self-starter.

You want to be whole, happy and successful.

You march to your own drummer.

Other people underestimate you and your abilities.

Misfortune and adversity are assailing you from every direction.

HOW TO FILL YOUR POCKETS, HEART AND LIFE WITH ABUNDANCE

The Abundance Creed asks nothing of you but belief in supernatural and divine supply. Once your power of belief is working its magic, you will be in touch with satisfaction, contentment, riches, plenty, abundance and everything you can desire, wish for, or dream of. The Abundance Creed (see page 177) opens the doors to happiness for you and then follows through by bringing that happiness to *you!* You don't have to do anything but *believe*.

Get revivified.

Get forward-looking.

Get hopeful.

Get free of lack and less.

Get out from under financial stress.

Get rid of monetary fears.

Get away from destitution and despondency.

Get miraculous aid from known and unknown quarters.

Get food, jobs, loves, money, riches, fun, and pleasure.

Get substantial and real help in your time of need.

Get others to come to your aid.

Get what you want out of life when others cannot.

Get your dollars multiplying into the thousands.

Get bill collectors off your back, chains of deprivation from
around your neck and shackles of poverty from around your
ankles.

Get all this and infinitely more by using the magical Abundance
Creed which opens wide the doors of the supernatural storehouse of
all good things.

Believe in abundance when it seems furthest from you. *Believe* in
plenty in the midst of want. *Believe* in success during obvious defeat.
Activate your power of belief and the Abundance Creed will work
miracles in your life.

HOW TO LATCH ONTO YOUR BRIGHT AND SHINING STAR

Go over the preceding chapter carefully. Find your own difficulty
or the one most like it, and practice the creed suitable to your case.
Let the powerful Unconscious know that you are attentive, receptive
and worthy of its help. Then sit back and wait for It to come to your
aid. Go forth *believing* and you go forth conquering.

Of all the cases I might draw upon to demonstrate the magical
powers of personal creeds, the case of a young man in Ohio is
exemplary. This particular person embraced the foregoing creeds
wholeheartedly and practiced them one by one while he was conva-
lescing after a particularly dreadful disease which crippled him for
months. He grew steadily better and wrote to me. He explained that
he "systematized the creeds," and used one a day until he had recited
them all and then started over again. This is how he wiled away long
and lonely hours of hospitalization and convalescence. It is the heart
of his letter to me which I wish to share with you here, for it clearly
shows the results of one man's power of belief. He wrote in part:

I *believe* in Joy, and sadness is foreign to me.
I *believe* in Truth, and falsehood does not plague me.

I *believe* in Good Fortune, and bad luck passes me by.
I *believe* in Love, and my friends are many.
I *believe* in Self-Confidence, and I will not be moved.
I *believe* in Health, and no disease will kill me.
I *believe* in Success, and failure is impossible.
I *believe* in Energy, and vitality is mine.
I *believe* in Sustenance, and my needs are met.
I *believe* in Purity, and people find me attractive.
I *believe* in Cosmic Power, and people seek my advice.
I *believe* in Guardianship, and I am protected from evil.
I *believe* in Magnetism, and others are glad to see me.
I *believe* in Mastery, and nothing dominates me.
I *believe* in Immutability, and I am a rock.
I *believe* in Harmony, and I am invulnerable to assault.
I *believe* in Progress, and I rise continually.
I *believe* in Abundance, and I am never destitute.
I *believe* in Higher-than-human agencies, and I rest upon that
  faith.

A PARTING WORD

They say that an author should not use himself as an example in a book, but I am going to bend that rule just a little in this particular case, because what I have to share with you only tends to validate the efficacy of the creeds presented in this book for your use.

I was almost finished with the final typing of this book when the mailman delivered an interesting and unexpected Mailgram. Synchronicity occurred—meaningful coincidence—for I *believe* that having immersed myself in the task of bringing all of these creeds together between two covers tended to set up strong psychic and Unconscious energy, which in turn *created* the presence of the Mailgram.

This Mailgram was from the publisher of this book—Parker Publishing Company—and it was concerned with a previous book I wrote for them—*Satan, Sorcery and Sex*. Like all authors I of course wish success for my works, and like other people I desire fame,

fortune and happiness. I need only share one line of the Mailgram
with you to show what I mean when I say to you: *believe*. That one
line is:

Getting many requests for TV and Radio appearances.
Urgently need your phone number.